TEKEBASH & SABA

Saba Alemayoh

TEKEBASH & SABA

Recipes and Stories from an East African Kitchen

Interlink Books
An imprint of Interlink Publishing Group, Inc.
Northampton, Massachusetts

When I opened my restaurant in Melbourne's Fitzroy in 2015, it was promoted and referred to as Ethiopian. We judged that to be a necessary compromise; most people know Ethiopia, far fewer are familiar with Tigray, one of the east African country's nine states, which are divided mostly along ethnic lines.

Likewise, the earliest vision for Tekebash & Saba *was an "Ethiopian" food book inspired, in part, by the restaurant's success. But as time passed, and the situation became more dire in Tigray, it was increasingly important that we differentiate and identify with our Tigrayness, if you like, first and foremost.*

I did not want to bend to the pressure to make my food, my mother's food, fit common Western perceptions about Ethiopian cuisine—like that if it wasn't spicy then it wasn't legit. The recipes in this book capture the true Tigrayan dining experience: there are no appetizers, mains, or desserts, simply dishes that are often shared as part of a communal banquet for all to enjoy.

This book is dedicated to the people of Tigray.

Special thanks to my mother, Tekebash, and sister, Sara.

እንኳዕ ካባኹም ተፈጠርኩ

SALAMAT

Prologue

Food seems to be the most tangible window into culture and the stories that make up a life. For us, it has always gone beyond simply sustenance. Food is revered in its own right, like music and dance. There are events around the preparation of food, not just the consumption. For large celebrations everyone comes together to peel tons of onions and make liters of honey wine. Women are firmly allocated to the coffee station, and some are simply invited to provide entertainment with sentences that always start with "Remember...."

Living so far from our homeland, there is an unwritten policy that when traveling to Tigray to visit family, you must empty your luggage of all clothing and fill it with as many spices as you can get past customs. We would try to make clandestine exits from Australia so that friends didn't plead with us to just bring back one or two kilos of shiro for them in our haul.

This idea inspired me to share my mother's kitchen with the Melbourne culinary scene in 2015 by opening Saba's Ethiopian Restaurant.

> ***This is not your regular cookbook! The recipes are the legacy of an extraordinary woman—my mother, Tekebash Gebre—born in Tigray in the shadows of the Aksumite dynasty, under the rule of the last Ethiopian emperor. Her formative years were spent under a communist regime before she fled to Sudan during a civil war that gripped the nation for 17 years.***

She has been on a migration journey ever since, but her heart continues to beat to the drums of Tigray. Despite having spent more time abroad than she has at home, she is unequivocally Tigraweyti. That is the complexity of identity and home: it cannot be captured by the status of your citizenship, but rather it is an intangible mark within your being.

She has worked with food in one way or another all her life, from landing her first job as a live-in cook in Khartoum, being a housewife, becoming a street-food vendor to raise a child, working as a kitchen hand in restaurants below minimum wage in Australia and being a head chef at her daughter's restaurant on one of Melbourne's most competitive hospitality strips. My mother not only worked with food but loved her children through it too. As I went through her door she would hold a utility bill in one hand, yelling at me to call them so they can explain why her bill was higher than it should be, which was followed immediately by, "What do you want to eat?"

> ***My mama's Tigray cuisine was developed in diaspora communities on her journey across continents. Sudanese food in particular has always been intertwined, with some dishes merged and some ingredients adopted into existing recipes, but some are kept distinctly separate.***

When we opened the restaurant, it was booked out for two weeks straight and won accolades beyond our imagination, from *The New York Times*, *Broadsheet,* and beyond. I tell you this to say that the woman is good, and potentially a pan-whisperer. Throughout the five years of running Saba's Ethiopian Restaurant, we never had a recipe book or any measuring equipment, simply her taste buds. I attempted to write the restaurant recipes down but my mother refused—she preferred to work without recipes. So, she cooked using her tongue and I managed front of house from the heart. Food is the way Tegaru show love and keep culture alive, and we wanted the food to be true to us.

We have now finally sat down together to write these recipes to share with you a delectable story, I suppose. I call this book *Tekebash & Saba*. Food is our familial cord to each other, and to home. It's a window into our story and that of Tegaru.

CONTENTS

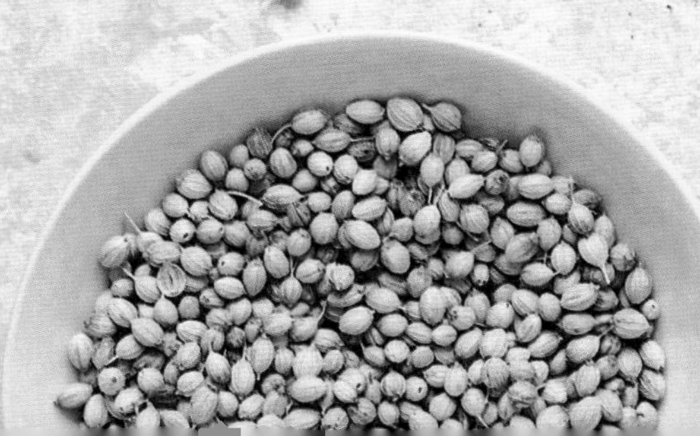

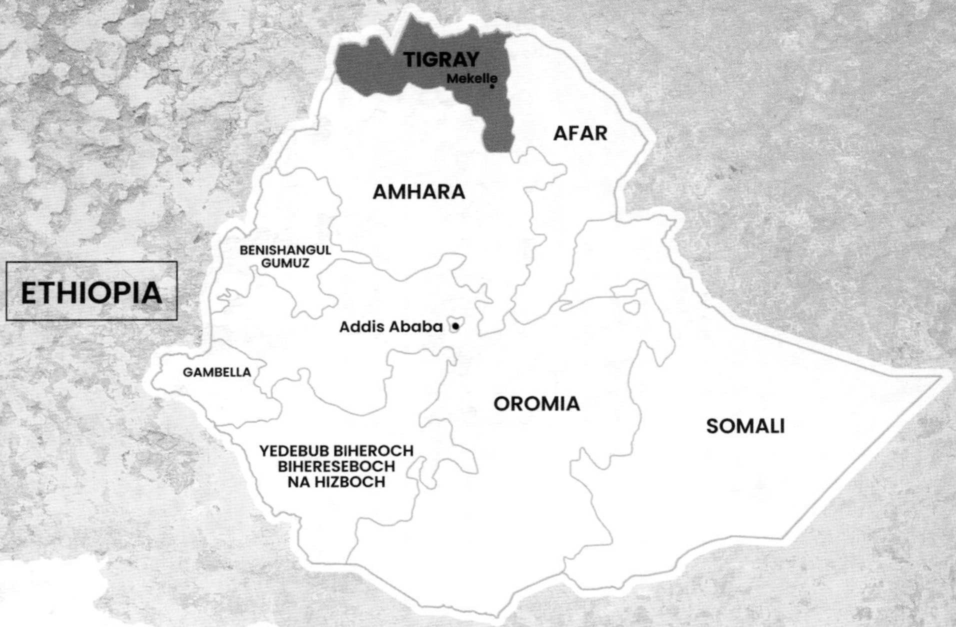
TIGRAY
Mekelle
AFAR
AMHARA
BENISHANGUL GUMUZ
ETHIOPIA
Addis Ababa
GAMBELLA
OROMIA
SOMALI
YEDEBUB BIHEROCH BIHERESEBOCH NA HIZBOCH

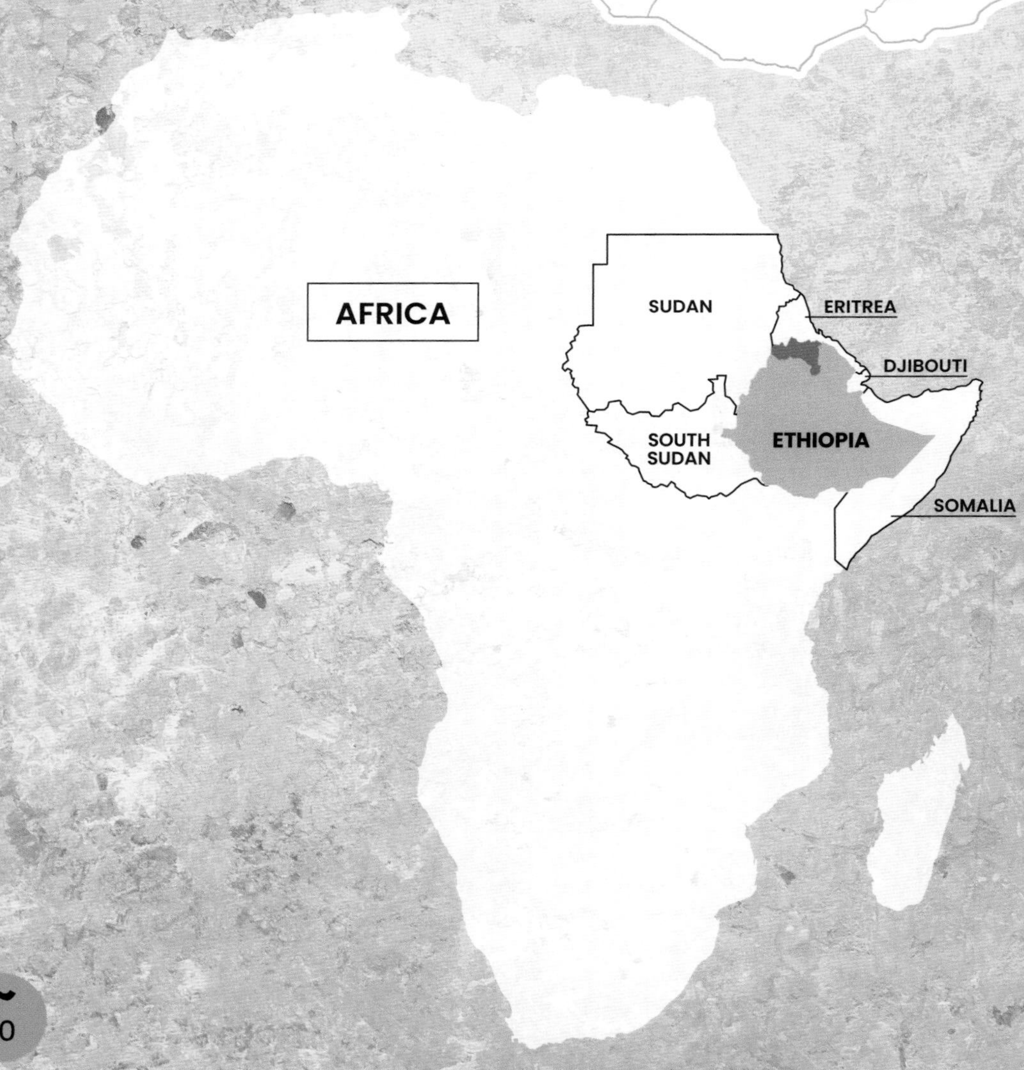
AFRICA
SUDAN
ERITREA
DJIBOUTI
SOUTH SUDAN
ETHIOPIA
SOMALIA

WHERE IS TIGRAY?

Tigray is the northernmost state of the Federal Democratic Republic of Ethiopia. Since 1991, Ethiopia has been a collective of nine states divided predominantly along ethnic lines. This division has been about balancing the need for self-determination while maintaining the border integrity of Ethiopia as a whole.

Ethiopia is made up of more than 80 different ethnicities, with almost an equal division between Islam and Christianity. It shares precariously managed borders with neighboring countries Somalia and Sudan, and is the only country in the region not to have been colonized by a European power. Certain groups—predominantly the Amhara and Tegaru (Semitic groups in the north)—have forcefully incorporated the south of modern-day Ethiopia. In addition, Ethiopian rulers made arrangements with Italy and England to claim masses of land that weren't ours from neighboring countries.

This is an attempt to give you the context of a region that is steeped in complex histories, and a civilization that can be traced back more than 2000 years.

It was a kingdom that had reached all the way to southern Arabia, was spoken about by Ancient Greeks and written about in the Bible, Koran, and beyond. Tigray was the first place to provide refuge for Islam, and the second in the world to make Christianity the official religion of the state.

> *The concept of being Ethiopian is a constructed one. To paraphrase author Chimamanda Ngozi Adichie, the only authentic identity for the African is the tribe; we became Ethiopian through conquests.*

The only consistency of our identity is our Tigrayness. Most Tegaru only begin to identify as Ethiopian when they leave their homeland. Let me give you some context: As a teenager in 2006, I went to visit family members in the villages of my homeland. I met a cousin of mine who was, at the time, 12 years old. He asked me "Do you speak Amharic in Australia?" (Amharic is the official language of Ethiopia.) I tell you this to demonstrate that the most foreign land and language he could envision was that of another tribe within the borders of Ethiopia. Urban Tegaru are worldlier, but more than 80 percent of Tegaru continue to live in regional areas, in varying degrees of isolation, and there are some areas that one can only access on foot. The Tegaru sense of locality is pronounced when we live there, but flattened when we leave.

I am writing this amid a genocide that is taking place against the people of Tigray at the hands of the Ethiopian Federal Government and its allies. This started on November 4th, 2020, and it continues to rage as I write this book.

The pretext used to justify the genocide has been multifaceted: an allegation by the Federal Government that North Command (a military base in Mekelle, in the Tigray region) was attacked by the Tigray state and/or that the state conducted elections against the Federal Government's embargo delaying elections due to COVID-19. The first allegation is disputed by the state of Tigray and the second justification appears ungrounded in jurisdiction. The official constitution of Ethiopia allows states to make decisions on state elections as it pleases, with the federal government having jurisdiction over federal matters.

> ***For a multitude of reasons, irrespective of politics, the relationship between the people of Tigray and the Federal Government disintegrated beyond diplomacy.***

Why this conflict started, and who is to blame, will make a great thesis topic for future generations; however, there are undisputed truths: there have been indiscriminate bombings of the civilian population and blockades of all supplies, electricity, telecommunication, and banking. More than 50,000 refugees have crossed the border to escape the war, millions are internally displaced, and the entire state is suffering the effects of man-made famine. Ethnic Tegarus have been stood down from all military positions (including foot soldiers) and civil positions in other regions, and Tegaru around the country are being arrested arbitrarily and having their assets seized.

Centering this book around Tigray food and cultural history is, in itself, a revolutionary act in honor of the strong lineage we come from. The absence of politics in one's life—even in something as simple as culinary culture—is a privilege not afforded to all.

> ***However, it is also important to acknowledge that Tigray cuisine doesn't exist in a vacuum, nor can I argue that it is extremely distinctive from our neighbors to the north and south. There are similarities within Ethiopian cuisine in general, and with Eritrean food.***

Tigrinya, the Tigray native language, is not only spoken, but has a script with a rich history that can be traced from Ge'ez, a language dating back to the third or fourth century CE, belonging to the Semitic family. Tigrinya in its current form appears in writing during the thirteenth century. The script has 32 letters, each having seven variations for different sounds. It's syllabic, with 224 symbols.

I am mentioning the complexity of the written language to ask you to pardon how I write the dishes in English. I must spell it phonetically as close as I can, while dealing with the shortcomings of the sounds available in English. I have attempted to replicate the titles as closely as I can.

*From left to right:
Saba Alemayoh, Tekebash
Gebre, and Sara Medhania.*

The backbone of the cuisine

Tigray's cuisine has three essential recipes that form the building blocks for most dishes: injera (fermented flatbread), tesmi (spiced butter), and berbere or dilik (powdered chile mix or paste).

The development of the cuisine has been influenced by faith and availability. Ninety-five percent of Tegaru are Orthodox Christians: as part of this we practice Lent and other fasting periods, eating exclusively vegan meals 180–210 days of the year, which has meant we've developed extensive vegan offerings.

When Lent has passed there is a strong preference for a heavy meat diet, with vegetable accompaniments rendered unnecessary. Both meat and veg as the backbone of meals, and the idea of three-course meals, are foreign concepts. Dessert is also not embedded in the cuisine.

The essential starch that accompanies all meals is injera, a spongy sour-tasting flatbread that doubles as a utensil with which we eat stews.

It is usually made with a grain called teff, which is one of the earliest grains to be cultivated in Tigray—as early as the third millennium BCE.

This hearty superfood is drought resistant and relatively easy to grow in the mountainous lands of Tigray. Teff is more closely related to other grasses in the lovegrass family than to the wheat family. Teff was exclusively found in Ethiopia and Tigray due to export bans that were in place until 2015. In 2003, in a partnership with the Ethiopian Institute of Biodiversity Conservation, Dutch agronomist Jans Roosjen was sent a variety of teff seeds for research and development. In 2007, a Dutch company obtained a patent for the exclusive production of teff. Essentially, this prevented the region from financially benefitting from one of its biggest assets—neo-colonialism at its best.

The grain is widely grown in three varieties: ivory, brown, and red. As a child I would hear my mom scream over the landline, using an international phone card bought from the local milk bar, asking, "How much is a kuntal (100 kilos) of teff now?" This is the barometer we use to gauge how the economy is going.

Given teff wasn't accessible, Tegaru became innovative with the grain they used to make injera, using sorghum, self-rising flour, and barley as substitutes. It can be easier to make injera with self-rising flour as it improves the fermentation; however, the taste tends to lack those tangy deep flavors.

Due to the demands of the Western world, most Tegaru women abroad have stopped making injera from scratch, opting instead for injera from local habesha bakeries that make it in bulk. My mother went back to making injera at home using teff when my sister was diagnosed with celiac disease.

Injera is served at room temperature with the dishes served hot on top. Women usually make the injera at the start of the day and let them sit until you're ready to eat.

INJERA *Fermented flatbread*

GF V VG

Makes 12

You'll need to start this recipe two days ahead, but most of that time you're just letting the fermentation happen. You will need woven mats for the injera to cool down on. These are usually available in Asian and African general purpose stores.

INGREDIENTS

7½ cups (1 kg) teff flour *(see tip)*

1 teaspoon instant yeast

6⅓ cups (1.5 liters) lukewarm water *(you may not end up using it all)*

METHOD

Stir the teff flour and yeast together—we traditionally do this by hand, but a stand mixer can also be used. Gradually add the water, taking breaks to knead the dough. Be careful you don't add too much water—it should be smooth and slightly sticky (like playdough), but not wet. Leave the mixture in an airtight container overnight in a warm place. Your kitchen counter or pantry will suffice.

The next day, add enough water to thin out the mixture to a pancake batter consistency. Cover and let it sit overnight again.

When you open it, a sour smell may be omitted and there may potentially be a dark layer that looks like mold. This is aerobic yeast. Discard the top layer of liquid. You will be left with a thick dough.

Bring 1 cup (250 ml) water to a boil in a small saucepan. Scoop ½ cup of the dough and stir it into the boiling water using a whisk. Make sure it's mixed really well. It will have the consistency of a milkshake.

Add this batter to the rest of the dough and mix very well. The batter's consistency should be between a pancake and crepe batter. Add more lukewarm water if you need it. This process ensures that the injera is soft. Cover and let it sit for 2 hours.

Place a nonstick frying pan (that has a lid) over medium heat and use a small jug (or ladle) to pour the mixture all around the pan. You want to make it thicker than a crepe but not as thick as a pancake. Leave it uncovered until half of the injera has tiny holes, then cover the pan with the lid for 5–10 seconds to steam-cook the top.

Gently use a butter knife to transfer the injera onto traditional woven mats. Leave the injera on their mats to cool, ensuring that you don't stack them as they will stick together.

Once cool, serve the injera as a base with stew on top and extra rolled injera on the side.

- One hundred percent teff can be hard to work with. You can supplement it by replacing 50 percent of the teff with sorghum or wheat flour.

Berbere and dilik

Berbere is often incorrectly translated as chile. The Portuguese brought chile to East Africa from South America in the fifteenth and sixteenth centuries.

From these original chiles came an indigenous variety, brown chile peppers, endemic to modern-day Ethiopia and Eritrea. These peppers are dried out and blended to create a unique chile mix, giving birth to berbere. It is a unique blend, combining more than 20 different spices ground up: coriander, cumin, green cardamom, whole cloves, turmeric, ginger, garlic, red chile, onion, salt, and many more.

Like Italians have tomato days, Tegaru households usually have berbere preparation days. It takes several days for women to wash, roast, and air-dry varied combinations of spices for milling.

Each area in Tigray has a local mill where the community can bring their own sack of spices early in the morning and line up around the corner waiting their turn. They watch their batch get milled and ensure the same batch is returned to them in the sack. Mothers would send batches to their urban working daughters. Of course, some women's mixtures are considered better than others. Even if the ingredients are the same, the taste can vary based on the winnowing, roasting, the measurements, and the quality of the raw ingredients. Berbere is difficult to make with limited access to communal mill houses, and so, dilik was born.

Unlike berbere, dilik is a paste rather than a powder, which allows you to use standard chile powder to create small batches that can be made easily.

You can buy berbere at habesha stores and African groceries, or make your own mixture. Use the spices listed for Dilik on page 25.

DILIK ድልኽ *Chile spice paste*

GF V VG

Makes about 1 lb 2 oz (500 g)

INGREDIENTS

1½ tablespoons (7.5 g) ground ginger

1 tablespoon (7.5 g) ajwain seeds

1 tablespoon (7.5 g) black sesame seeds

1 tablespoon (7.5 g) coriander seeds

¾ tablespoon (7.5 g) cardamom seeds

1 tablespoon (7.5 g) korarima (Ethiopian cardamom)

2½ tablespoons (25 g) garlic powder

2½ tbsp (25 g) onion flakes

scant 2 cups (250 g) chile powder (Kashmir or medium)

2 tablespoons (35 g) table salt

½ cup (125 ml) sunflower oil

METHOD

Using a dry nonstick frying pan over medium heat, roast all the dry ingredients except for the chile powder and salt, until the aromas go out. This should take approximately 5 minutes. Tip them onto a plate and leave to cool down.

Once cooled, use a blender to grind the spices into a smooth, fine texture.

Transfer this mixture to a food processor, add the chile powder and salt, and mix the ingredients well.

Add 1½ cups (350 ml) water and the oil and mix until it's firm and looks like playdough.

Put in a container with a tight-fitting lid and store in the fridge for up to 1 year.

- When using this mixture, scoop it out using a dry spoon and avoid double-dipping to ensure your paste doesn't go bad.

TESMI ጠስሚ *Spiced butter*

GF V

Makes about 3 cups (750 ml)

Spiced butter is used predominantly when cooking meat dishes and can be made using margarine if you are vegan.

INGREDIENTS

2 teaspoons fenugreek seeds

2 teaspoons cardamom seeds

3 cups (700 g) unsalted butter

½ red onion, coarsely chopped

5 garlic cloves, crushed

1 teaspoon ground turmeric

METHOD

In a dry frying pan over medium heat toast the fenugreek seeds until they are a light brown color.

Grind the fenugreek and cardamom seeds in a grinder for a few seconds, until coarsely ground.

Melt the butter in a saucepan over the lowest heat.

Add all the ingredients to the pan and stir for 15–20 minutes until the onion and garlic become brown.

Remove from the heat and let it sit until it cools down but doesn't solidify. Strain the butter into a dry container. This will last for months in the fridge.

THE FIRST DISH SHE EVER COOKED

My mother was the youngest of a large brood of 12, with nine surviving to adulthood. Coming from such a big family meant that she didn't have to take on too many domestic chores since there were many hands on deck.

My grandmother was giving birth to my mother while her eldest kids were having their first children. By the time she was about 10 years old, my mother's elder brother was married and, of course, the new daughter-in-law was helping with the domestic chores. So, instead of participating in the chores, my mother was responsible for looking after the animals.

Generally, the women would make the injera in the morning either for the day or for a couple of days. Then they would make stews when the time came for lunch or for dinner—the lack of cold storage might have had something to do with it. Dry goods were stored in a cylinder made out of clay in the house, called qofo (ቆፎ). Honey, for those who had it, remained in the hive and was extracted as necessary.

Milk was only available if there was a cow calving—and then, you guessed it, it went from the cow's udder to your cup. I guess it's farm-to-plate before it was a trend. They even used the hand-operated stone mill to grind grains and legumes.

Agricultural science in Tigray has prevailed without modification for thousands of years, harvesting the same land over and over again, with most produce being consumed at the farm household level. Farms continue to use ox-plough cultivation of predominantly cereal crops.

One day my grandma wasn't around and my grandpa came home earlier than expected. My mom decided to make a very basic chickpea stew.

> ***Here, I must make a disclaimer that I ask you to heed for the remainder of the book. We use the word "stew" liberally to describe any cooked-down saucy concoction. Sometimes our stews are similar to dips, or even soups, but they are consumed as a stew on a bed of injera nonetheless.***

So, she made abesh. Her father ate it despite it being extremely salty. My grandma, a traditional, old-school woman, came home and told my grandpa that's what he gets for sending daughters to school. Go figure! After that, my mother didn't really cook beyond a handful of times until she found herself away from home in Khartoum.

ABESH ኣብሽ *Chickpea stew*

GF V VG

Serves 4

Certain ingredients are simply the superstars of Tigray cooking and chickpeas are one of these. Abesh is less spicy than its Shiro counterpart (page 39) and is the baked beans equivalent for farmsteads. Homes usually have dried chickpeas, and women simply grind them by hand and get cooking. Shiro requires them to have already spiced the chickpea flour beforehand.

INGREDIENTS

1⅔ cups (200 g) chickpea flour (besan)

1 small onion, finely diced

5 garlic cloves, peeled and minced

1 cup (250 ml) hot water

salt

sunflower oil, for cooking

Injera *(page 21)* **or toasted bread and fresh green chiles, to serve**

METHOD

In a food processor, combine the chickpea flour with 3 cups (750 ml) water, then blend. The mixture should reach a cream-like consistency. Set aside.

Sauté the onion, with just enough sunflower oil to keep it from sticking, in a pot over medium heat until translucent. Then add the garlic and cook for 1 minute.

Add the chickpea flour mixture to the pot and use a whisk to mix.

Add the hot water and keep whisking. It will get thicker as you keep cooking. It should be the consistency of a milkshake by the end. Add salt to taste. This should take approximately 7 minutes.

Leave it over medium heat to bubble for 30 minutes. Cover the pot to avoid a mess!

Serve with injera or toasted bread with a side of fresh green chiles. Alternatively, you can simply enjoy it like a soup.

VEGAN SCRAMBLED EGGS

Chickpea scramble

GF V VG

Serves 2

This simple and delicious dish was a staple on the farm during Lent.

INGREDIENTS

1 cup (120 g) chickpea flour (besan)

½ teaspoon salt

½ red onion, diced

sunflower oil or margarine, for cooking

2 garlic cloves, freshly crushed

1 green bell pepper, diced

1 small red chile, finely diced (optional)

Toasted bread, to serve

METHOD

Put the chickpea flour and salt in a food processor with ½ cup (125 ml) water and blend until combined well.

Transfer to a nonstick saucepan and bring the mixture to a boil while stirring. Reduce the heat and keep stirring using a wooden spoon, creating a playdough-like consistency but in larger chunks. There is a tendency for the mixture to stick so keep stirring.

Sauté the onion in oil or margarine in a frying pan until translucent, then add the garlic and bell pepper and fry until soft.

Add the chickpea mixture to the pan and stir thoroughly. Add the red chile, if using, and mix thoroughly. Serve warm with toasted bread.

Education during a civil war

Literacy rates in Tigray, and Ethiopia as a whole, were quite low in the 1980s, but literacy of 51 percent was achieved by 2017.

In 1950, Ethiopia had 620 elementary schools and enrolled just over 50,000 students—a very small proportion of school-age kids. At the time Ethiopia had a population of 18 million. Most of the schools were concentrated in the capital city (Amhara region at the time) and Eritrea. This was due to a combination of discriminatory government policy and Italian colonization of Eritrea.

My mom grew up in Adi Kuhla, which is part of the Aksum district—the fourth largest city in Tigray. She went to a school in Daego, which went up to grade 8, approximately 40 minutes' walk one way, with some kids walking 2 hours to get there. Most kids in rural areas commenced primary school later to ensure they were capable of making the trek, the youngest around 9 years old and eldest around 14 being reasonable for the time. Going to school was a privilege, as some families considered the expense of stationery, kerosene lights used to study at night, and sacrificing the extra hand on the farm as indulgent. Female children were also less likely to be able to balance the demands of domestic chores within the family, or potential early marriage, leading to higher dropout rates relative to boys.

Due to the civil war that was going on (between 1974–1991), schools were being closed and opened on a regular basis. This was particularly the case for regional towns, like Daego, that were Tigray People's Liberation Front (TPLF) strongholds. The cities of Tigray were more consistently under the communist Mengistu regime from Addis Ababa.

So, my mom's parents decided it was time for her to board with her brother in Aksum in grade 4. Boarding with family in other towns was common practice.

Her two elder sisters had also boarded there before being sent to Addis Ababa to live with their aunt. At that point this was the only member of her immediate or extended family who had left the Tigray region or even the Aksum area.

At that time, my mother's family would have been considered working class or lower middle class, relative to the area; however, this did not release them from very tightly managed household budgets. The culture around boarding was for parents to provide sinqi to cover the additional cost of extra children in the household. Sinqi wasn't dollar for dollar per se, but rather a portion of farmed goods (grains, spices, and legumes) the family could afford. My mother would go to her parents every weekend (a 1.5 hour walk each away) and return carrying sinqi on her back.

> *Regardless, it was considered a great privilege for your family to commit to your education at the expense of a helping hand on the farm and for you to have a place to board in town.*

This lack of educational infrastructure outside of the Amhara regions contributed to the discontentment around the way the region was deliberately being underdeveloped by the centralist government of Ethiopia.

SHIRO POWDER AND SHIRO STEW ሽሮ

Spiced chickpea powder and chickpea stew

GF V VG

The average Tigraweyti family would have shiro daily: it was cheap and accessible. However, the flavors within it are nothing to snub your nose over—it's absolutely delicious. In the eighties and nineties, Tigray and Ethiopia as a whole was devastated by the HIV epidemic and there were advertisements everywhere for condoms and the prevention of HIV. Most older folks had no grasp on what it was, but all were scared of the devastating effects.

One day my cousin asked my aunt what's for lunch today and she said "shiro" and he said to her, "I don't know if you've heard, but they are saying shiro can give you HIV" and she didn't miss a beat and responded, "Well, we will have to eat it with a condom because shiro is not negotiable." This is how strongly we feel about shiro! To be frank, I don't believe she or the community really understood what HIV was or how it was transmitted, since literacy levels were quite low and the conservative nature of the culture prevents open discussion about sex education.

This recipe makes a very generous amount, but given it takes several steps to make, it's worth making a big batch to enjoy over time. If you'd prefer to make a smaller amount, feel free to divide the quantities. ›

SHIRO POWDER AND SHIRO STEW ሽሮ

Spiced chickpea powder and chickpea stew

GF V VG

Makes 10 cups (1.25 kg) powder / Stew serves 2

INGREDIENTS

SHIRO POWDER (see tip)

2½ cups (500 g) dried chickpeas

2¼ cups (500 g) peeled yellow split peas

5½ oz (150 g) dried chiles

2 tablespoons (25 g) dried garlic powder

¼ cup (25 g) ground ginger

2½ tablespoons (25 g) dried onion

2 tablespoons (35 g) coarse sea salt

scant ½ cup (10 g) dried basil

heaped 1 tablespoon (12 g) cardamom seeds

heaped 1 tablespoon (12 g) rue seeds

SHIRO STEW

½ onion, diced

1 teaspoon minced garlic

sunflower oil, for cooking

½ teaspoon salt

1 cup (120 g) Shiro powder *(see left)*

Injera *(page 21)*, **to serve**

METHOD

For the shiro powder, roast the chickpeas and yellow split peas in a large, dry nonstick frying pan for 10–15 minutes, or until a nice golden brown color. Set aside.

Separately, roast the spices for 1–2 minutes in a dry frying pan.

After all the spices have cooled, mix everything together in a big bowl. Use a food processor to grind the mixture in batches to a smooth flour consistency.

When the whole mixture has been ground, transfer to an airtight container. At room temperature, it can be stored for 4–5 months. If stored in the freezer, it can last up to 1 year.

To make shiro stew, sauté the onion and garlic in oil in a small saucepan. Use just enough oil to keep the onion from sticking.

Once translucent, add 2½ cups (625 ml) water and the salt to the pan and bring to a boil. Slowly add the shiro powder and use a whisk to keep it nice and smooth. Once you have mixed the shiro powder enough that there are no lumps, reduce the heat to medium, put the lid on, and let it cook for another 10 minutes. The mixture will get thicker as you keep it on the stove. It has a tendency to pop everywhere, so placing a lid on the pan will be a good idea.

- You can easily halve or double this recipe. You can also buy ready-made shiro powder at a habesha grocery or online and skip the entire first part of this recipe.

S’NIGH ስንግ *Stuffed green chiles*

GF V VG

Serves 4

It is common for us to eat vegan foods with fresh green chile—we take bites in between morsels. Chile powders and pastes are generally the preferred accompaniment for meat dishes. This stuffed green chile is an occasional one that Mom only makes when guests are coming. Serve it alongside Shiro stew (page 40).

INGREDIENTS

½ red onion, finely chopped

½ tomato, finely chopped

1 teaspoon olive oil

1 teaspoon lemon juice

½ teaspoon salt

6 green chiles

METHOD

Mix the onion, tomato, olive oil, lemon juice, and salt in a bowl.

Split the chiles lengthways on one side, keeping the stems, and scrape out the seeds.

Use a spoon to stuff the green chiles with the onion mixture, and close back up.

Serve with shiro.

FLEEING TIGRAY

My mother was born during the final few years of the last emperor of Ethiopia's rule. By the time she was six years old, he had been overthrown by a military coup in 1974, which was motivated by a mismanaged ecological disaster that left hundreds of thousands starving and country folk leaving their homesteads to come to towns with no national relief in sight.

> *The Capital denied the existence of the famine and truck drivers were retelling the horrific scenes they witnessed in rural areas.*

The monarch was replaced by a Marxist–Leninist government (the Derg) led by Major Mengistu Haile Mariam. Mengistu's reign was plagued with instability: war with Somalia, insurgencies for independence in Eritrea. Tigray was rebelling against discriminatory policies from Addis, the Ethiopian capital, which introduced land reforms that disproportionately affected the region, along with a lack of development, mishandling of drought, and the suppression of language and culture. This was exacerbated by the Red Terror campaign and the aerial bombardment supported by the USSR—as Ethiopia was aligned with the communist block during the Cold War.

> *Mengistu was the originator of the phrase "Ethiopia Tikdem," Ethiopia First. He instigated assimilation policies in line with the dominant culture (Amhara); impractical policies for a country that has more than 80 different ethnicities and language groups within its national borders.*

This discontent created the fertilizer for the anti-Derg revolution, Second Woyane, giving birth to three different armed-struggle movements: Ethiopian Democratic Union (EDU), Ethiopian People's Revolutionary Democratic Front (EPRPDF), and Tigray People's Liberation Front (TPLF). My mother remembers extrajudicial killings for perceived misconduct or for supporting Woyane—the bodies would be left displayed in the Daero market of Aksum. No one was allowed to cover the bodies or bury them, they were to be examples to others. Some people were killed at their front door, leaving the families to discover their bodies. Tegaru went to administration offices in their own region and were required to speak in Amharic, and thus needed to use an interpreter to make simple government requests; schools stopped teaching Tigrinya, the native language of the area. Senior government administrators were sent from Addis to the region to help with the assimilation process.

These encounters with the Derg regime led to grassroots support for the armed struggle.

The TPLF emerged as the dominant party and became a part of the Ethiopian coalition government. TPLF was founded from a radical student movement with the goal of bringing about class revolution to dismantle Amhara elitism, and to create ethnic equality through federation. Early on, TPLF understood the movement needed to be grassroots in order to win the hearts and minds of the populace. TPLF had a very disciplined force in contrast to the Derg government; they never confiscated goods or crops, always paid for what they wanted, refrained from alcohol, and put a ban on consensual sex between their forces and civilians. Borrowing from Mao's politics, TPLF persecuted its fighters harshly for crimes against the populace.

TPLF's main philosophy was about development, armed struggle, and eradicating illiteracy simultaneously, with a motto that translated to "weapon, plough, and pen in hand." In practice, soldiers were participating in improving agricultural practices and projects, and running makeshift schools under trees in rural areas. By 1983, TPLF was looting enough weapons from the Ethiopian army to adequately begin training its own fighters. TPLF had strong support in Tigray. Militarily it was able to hold regional areas, with the cities being dominated by the Derg regime. This was due to the inaccessible terrain of Tigray and the strong grassroots support they enjoyed within the regional population.

The small regional towns would change hands throughout this period regularly, as the Derg government would periodically attempt to stamp out TPLF-controlled areas. My mother's home village was a TPLF stronghold, with her brother as the regional organizer, and she boarded with her other brother in Aksum (a stronghold of the Derg regime) for school. She, like many others, had to commute back and forth between the two forces with checkpoints in between.

Derg conducted one of their many raids at my uncle's place in the country. His wife was at home with her toddler, and she was marshalled to accompany the soldiers to Axum with her child on her back and her whole herd of cattle. While she was in the custody of Derg soldiers, a battle broke out with TPLF forces and two Derg soldiers were killed. In retaliation, a soldier came over to my aunt and broke her arm with the buttstock of his rifle. He sent her back with her baby attached to her back and confiscated the cattle. She couldn't walk all the way to Adi Kuhla, one-and-a-half hours away, so she walked to my aunt's place 30 minutes away. They placed a makeshift splint on her arm and insisted that she go to the hospital through a different checkpoint as they didn't believe the fracture would heal on its own. After being hospitalized for two days, having left her other two children and the farmstead alone with my uncle in hiding, she was anxious to return home.

> ***My mom was my aunt's caretaker while she was in hospital, even though she was only 15 or 16 at the time. My aunt asked my mom to take her back to the farm and that's what she did.***

They had not obtained the right approval for her to leave the hospital—difficult because she was the wife of a TPLF organizer—and soldiers were sent to summon my mother to court. As the soldiers were escorting her to court, one of them kept hurling abuse that my mom was anti-revolution and good for nothing, a spy and so on. My mother was a hot-tempered teenager who had come of age with gunfire right outside her home. Her family home was repeatedly raided and herds of cattle were taken on a regular basis. In that moment she remembered thinking "You're probably going to kill me anyway, so I may as well go down in flames," so she hurled abuse right back at them.

By this point, it had begun to get extremely difficult to stay out of the gunsights of the Derg regime and remain out of the fray, and Tegaru soon saw revolting as the only option, whether it be by joining the armed forces in hordes, seeking refuge in Sudan, or creating civil disobedience.

Luckily for my mom, it wasn't her day. She was taken to court and they sent for her guardian to represent her on two charges: taking a patient out of hospital without the right paperwork and verbal assault on a soldier. Coincidentally, the judge was Tigrayan and he told them off the record, "She has a hot temper and we are living in dangerous times: you need to advise her to tame that tongue in order to keep breathing." This experience, in addition to the constant disruption to school, curfews, gunshots, raids, and now the attention of local soldiers made my mom feel that staying in Aksum was no longer an option. The daily hushed conversations among the youth were filled with who had left to join the armed struggle or go abroad. Translated directly, the word used was not "left" but "lost." I find this translation interesting, as Tigrinya language has a word for "left," but they always used "lost." Those who left didn't want to go, but had no choice, and I guess they could sense they would never come back. Nonetheless, leaving was illegal during the Derg regime and if you were caught you risked prosecution or death.

My mom had a cousin the same age as her, and they spoke about leaving but the cousin kept dragging her feet saying she wanted to wait until the birth of a niece, or until she saw a family member from the regional area one more time, and so on. My mother started to get nervous that they would get busted or her cousin might tell someone. There was an immense amount of distrust amongst Tegaru as members of the same family might be in the underground TPLF group or in the Derg spy network (referred to as Banda). My mom decided to leave without her cousin, and left under the guise of going to school.

During that time, Tegaru were fleeing in hordes. They would walk to the regional areas, connect with TPLF forces, and flee with them to Sudan as an attaché. When my mother reached the forces, they did a brief vetting to check she wasn't a spy, then allocated her to a troop. Refugees were given basic instructions on how to conduct themselves in the battlefield—don't wear bright colors, no fraternization of any kind, no cooking during the day, and only walk at night to avoid aerial bombardment.

> *The human caravan would move from town to town through battlefields, the journey to Sudan taking anywhere between three and four months.*

Most of the journey was on foot, walking up to nine hours a night. My mother had joined from the Aksum region, while others would join from their respective places. Sudan is due west from Aksum, and the journey they took was based on military objectives, but also acted as a recruitment drive of sorts for TPLF. As a result, the journey for the refugees might include a political conference in the south-east, or a tour to see agricultural development organized by TPLF in the north, and so on. The commute was free of charge, but risky as you were an attachment to a troop engaged in a battle.

> *Many of the refugees that started the journey with my mom chose to join the armed struggle instead of heading to Sudan.*

She continued on, choosing to be a part of the external battlefield. The TPLF always encouraged those who left to maintain strong links with home. They understood that revolutions were not secured on the battlefield alone but in all walks of society by winning the hearts and minds of the populace. There were no conscripts throughout the 17-year struggle; they had to convince the population, town by town, individual by individual, that there could be a better tomorrow and they could all participate in whatever capacity they wanted to. The collective felt they had a part to play in the revolution—those who left were empowered to view fundraising and lobbying as a revolutionary act. Teachers were told that eradicating illiteracy was a revolutionary act. People truly saw themselves as having a part to play in the armed struggle.

The war ended in 1991. A coalition of multi-ethnic insurgents led by TPLF with Meles Zenawi Asres as a president entered Addis Ababa unopposed. By July, Eritrea was granted independence with no resistance. During that period a democratic constitution was drafted and a federation of nine states divided along major ethnic lines emerged, with a great degree of self-determination and the right to secede if the Federation became unworkable written into the Ethiopian constitution.

On November 4th, 2020, history repeated itself with the declaration of war against Tigray. Six months of indiscriminate aerial bombardments of civil infrastructure, looting, and systemic displacement has left 4.5 million out of 5.7 million Tegaru in need of food.

> *By March 15th, 2021, barely one out of 10 health facilities were functioning, due to targeted looting by Ethiopian and Eritrean armies in Tigray.*

According to Médecins Sans Frontières (MSF), there were confirmed reports of the use of sexual violence to subjugate the region. Within two months of the war, more than 60,000 refugees fled to Sudan, with more than half being women and children. In a decade or two, there will be a Tegaru scraping together of fragments of home and culture in a foreign land. Another mother will teach her children about a culture gripped so tightly, and that is the sad cycle of life.

> *One of the main foods my mom remembers eating repeatedly while on the move was kicha. This was effective as it was not onerous to make, used few ingredients, did not need fermentation, and any flour would do.*

KICHA ቅጫ *Flatbread*

V VG

Serves 4

INGREDIENTS

2 cups (300 g) wholewheat or all-purpose flour

pinch of salt

½ teaspoon instant yeast

1¼ cups (300 ml) warm water

METHOD

Combine all the ingredients in a bowl and mix well. Cover and let it sit for 1½—2 hours.

Put the mixture in a large nonstick frying pan and spread it out with your hands, or a ladle if you prefer. Cover the pan with a lid and cook over medium heat for around 7 minutes on each side, or until a charred crust has formed.

Depending on the size of your pan, you may need to work in batches. Take it off the heat and leave to cool.

Cut into pieces and serve with Silsi *(page 54)* for breakfast, or serve with honey and tea as a snack.

SILSI ሰልሲ *Tomato sauce*

GF V

Makes about 1⅔ cups (400 ml)

This is a sauce that people might make as an accompaniment to less spicy vegetarian dishes. It's also great to use as a dip with Kicha (page 53). This is Tigray's Napoletana sauce.

INGREDIENTS

4 ripe tomatoes

1 cup (25 g) basil leaves

1 teaspoon salt, plus extra to taste

2 onions, finely diced

oil, for cooking

6 garlic cloves, finely diced

3 tablespoons Dilik *(page 25)*

heaped 1 tablespoon Tesmi *(page 26)*

Kicha *(page 53)* **or gluten-free flatbread, for dipping**

METHOD

Roast the tomatoes over an open flame on the stovetop using tongs until they start to blacken (you can also do this under the broiler). When cool enough to handle, peel off and discard the skins.

Put the tomatoes, basil, and salt in a food processor and blend to a paste consistency.

In saucepan set over medium heat, sauté the onion in oil until translucent then add the garlic and sauté for a minute.

Add the dilik and sauté for another minute (you may need to add some water to ensure it doesn't stick to the pan). Once the ingredients are mixed well, add the tomato mixture.

Add ½ cup (125 ml) water, cover with the lid, and let it simmer over low heat for 10 minutes, stirring every couple of minutes.

Add the tesmi and cook for another 5 minutes. Taste for seasoning and add more salt if needed. Serve with kicha.

- You can use this as a base for a vegetable stew or as a base for bolognese. You simply add chopped vegetables to the mixture and cook.

FIR FIR OR FIT FIT ፍርፍር OR ፍትፍት

Shredded flatbread with tomato sauce

V

Serves 2

This dish is called Fir fir when made with kicha, and Fit fit when made with injera. When made with kicha, you can eat it with a spoon. For fit fit, it is served on a bed of injera. The injera is used as a utensil to grab the fit fit mixture. This is usually enjoyed as a breakfast dish.

INGREDIENTS

1 small cucumber, chopped

1 tomato, chopped

1 green chile, chopped

¼ red onion, finely chopped

1 teaspoon olive oil

½ teaspoon salt

¼ cup (60 ml) freshly squeezed lemon juice

1 teaspoon vinegar

1 cup (220 g) Silsi *(page 54)*

2 cups (500 g) shredded Kicha *(page 53)*, **for Fir fir**

Injera *(page 21)*, **for Fit fit**

METHOD

Mix the cucumber, tomato, chile, and onion in a bowl.

In another small bowl, mix the olive oil, salt, lemon juice, and vinegar.

Put the silsi in a third bowl, and mix in the kicha, if making as fir fir.

Combine the cucumber mixture and oil mixture with the silsi mixture to serve.

Learning to cook in transit

Most Tegaru who fled the conflict in the 1980s fled with the logistical support of Tigray People's Liberation Front (TPLF). The TPLF usually brought the refugees to the bureau in Khartoum, Sudan's capital.

Newcomers would arrive with not a penny to their names and just the clothing on their backs. The office not only served as a welcoming hub for fleeing refugees, but a conference hall where they would hear news of what was happening in Tigray, receive letters from home, transfer money back to Tigray, and fundraise for the war efforts. As newcomers arrived, they would sleep and eat in the office until proper accommodation could be found. There were army forces of volunteers cooking to feed hundreds of people coming in and out of the office. Payment was optional, with newcomers being fed for free and those with work paying what they could afford.

As a newcomer came in, an announcement would be made of their name, the region they came from, and family lineage, and established members would be asked if they had space for someone to board with them for free. It wasn't uncommon to run into a person you went to school with, a relative, or someone from your town. The hosts would orientate their fellow country folk to the Sudanese laws, show them around, and help get them a job. Some of these houses were densely packed, with 10 people to a room being common practice. It was a "kumbaya" environment, with people predominately under the age of 25 bound together by the trauma of fleeing war.

Tegaru and other refugees from the Horn of Africa generally became the class of maids, cooks, gatemen, street traders, groundskeepers, and nannies for middle-class Sudanese families and non-governmental organization (NGO) workers living in the country.

My mother started working as a live-in maid and cook four months after she arrived. She spoke no Arabic (the dominant language in Khartoum), nor did she know how to cook; however, the women of the house generally did not work outside of the home, so were able to train their new maids to cook and hovered over them to ensure that cleaning standards were met. So, I guess my mother learned to cook Sudanese food from her various bosses.

> *The first dish her boss taught her was bamya (okra). She had never seen this vegetable in Tigray, nor had she eaten it. She remembers being so turned off by the slimy nature of it that she refused to eat it. Now it's a part of her regular cooking repertoire.*

My mother sent a portion of her first paycheck back home to her dad. She received a letter a month later from him, saying something along the lines of: "How did you come across so much money? I haven't spent it yet and the family is not in need of money and I hope you haven't earned it in a way has brought shame to the family." There was this fear in families back home that their children would become morally corrupt in order to survive. There was always honor in what my grandfather—and the community at large—called "honorable poverty": it was more important that you have a morally clean name than it was to be wealthy.

BAMYA *Okra*

GF

Serves 6

You can leave out the lamb to make this dish vegan.

INGREDIENTS

3 onions, finely diced

sunflower oil, for cooking

1 teaspoon crushed garlic (preferably fresh)

2½ oz (70 g) Dilik *(page 25)*

2½ cups (600 g) diced tomatoes

½ teaspoon ground cumin

1 lb 2 oz (500 g) diced lamb (approx. ¾ inch/2 cm chunks)

1 lb 2 oz (500 g) okra

salt

METHOD

In a pot, sauté the onion in sunflower oil over medium heat until soft. Add the garlic and sauté until translucent.

Add the dilik and turn the heat down to low. Keep stirring, adding water as necessary to stop it sticking.

Add the tomato and cumin and cook until the tomatoes are soft. It should take approximately 15 minutes.

Add the meat, stir, then add enough water to submerge the meat. Increase the heat to medium and cook for approximately 20 minutes, until tender.

While the meat cooks, chop the okra. You want to cut off both ends of the okra and chop it to the same size as the meat.

Once the meat is almost cooked—about 5 minutes away—add the okra and salt to taste. Cook for 5–7 minutes, just until the okra is tender. Avoid overcooking the okra, as it has a tendency to become slimy.

Serve with Ruz *(page 64)* or breadsticks.

RUZ *Rice*

GF V VG

Serves 2

Rice is not indigenous to Ethiopia nor is it a staple. It is a relatively new grain and was introduced in the 1970s. Rice is still absent in the average Tigraweyti diet. Still, this recipe is a great accompaniment for dishes such as Bamya (page 63) and other stews for when you don't have any injera on hand.

INGREDIENTS

1 cup (200 g) basmati rice

heaped 1 tablespoon finely chopped yellow onion

oil, for cooking

1 teaspoon minced garlic

½ teaspoon ground turmeric

1 teaspoon salt

METHOD

Wash the rice until the water is clear, then drain any excess water.

Sauté the onion in oil in a saucepan over medium heat until translucent.

Add the garlic and sauté for another minute. Add the turmeric and a small quantity of water to create a thick paste.

Add the drained rice and stir to coat the grains all over. Pour in 2 cups (500 ml) water and add the salt. Bring to a simmer. Reduce the heat and cook for 15 minutes with the lid on, or until the rice is tender and the water has been absorbed.

- You can also cook the rice using homemade lamb stock instead of water for a great flavor.

WEDDING? NO. MARRIED? YES!

Marriage, in my mother's generation, was a carefully curated arrangement made between two families, rather than the outcome of falling in love. Child marriage was a common practice; four of my six aunties were married by 12 years of age. Consummation of the marriage was supposed to be delayed until a girl came of age, denoted by her monthly flower (menstruation). Of course, compliance was based on cultural pressures and was not guaranteed.

It was considered important for the girl bride to be well assimilated with her in-laws, as she would most likely be moving to live in their proximity. The groom's family usually gave the newlyweds land and money to build their home, and the bride's family gave cattle. Given the couple usually went from their parents' home to their marital home, the two families took the responsibility of setting up the couple. The young girl would be raised between her in-laws and her parents until she came of age, spending months at a time at each house. It was considered a good opportunity for her to learn how the husband's mother ran her household to ensure she did it the same way. God forbid the man had to adapt to a different cooking style! Child marriage has been outlawed in Ethiopia, but continues to a limited degree. Urban Tegaru married slightly older: the arrangements were still made by the two families, with dating openly pre-engagement considered racy.

Arranged marriages were made based on your families' lineage and economic or class standing, coupled with an analysis of how well the matriarchs and patriarchs of your household upheld their duties. The process was more of a business transaction between the two families rather than the outcome of romance.

Weddings are a multi-day affair: in the regional areas there would be a wedding at the bride's house for her family and friends, and only the groom with his groomsmen would attend. Another would take place at the groom's house, and only the bride and her bridesmaids would attend. Preparation for the wedding is, in itself, a celebratory event in which the whole community will come to raise a tent for the wedding, slaughter the beasts, and make all the arrangements. It's customary to be given blessings along the lines of "God willing I look forward to cooking and dancing at your wedding." It is considered an honor to be able to help your loved ones during their wedding preparation. Food and alcohol preparation for a wedding would commence months before the wedding day. Women would make berbere mixes, date beers, and honey wines.

> *The wedding is followed by a period in which the couple go from one family to another, invited to dine by all their family and friends. I guess this is equivalent to a honeymoon period, but it's more like a ceremonial tour.*

Traditionally, all weddings had prenuptial agreements drawn up with the support of marriage guardians, irrespective of the value of their assets. Marriage guardians were like family-friend elders who would negotiate on each party's behalf and help navigate any future grievances that could not be resolved between the couple. Divorces were also clinical, with each party walking away with what they came with and all assets earned together—including, in regional areas, cattle born during the marriage—split fifty-fifty.

Second marriages are treated a little bit differently. It's usually discouraged to have children from the first marriage live with the couple unless both parties have children. Each party would leave children from their first marriage to be raised by their grandparents. It was considered ill-advised for children to grow up with step-parents, placing strain on a new marriage. If the man has three children and the woman two, the man may leave one child behind and bring two into the marriage like the woman—very clinical. However, keeping a marriage together took the effort of a whole community, including extended family and marriage guardians.

Divorce can be initiated by either party; however, it is customary to have mediation with your marriage guardians prior to proceeding with a divorce.

The sanctity of marriage and the coming together of two families disintegrated as young Tegaru refugees found themselves geographically dislocated without the extended family framework to uphold culture and tradition. A great number of young people came of age during the conflict and were the first generation to leave Tigray. These young people now found themselves also being the first generation to negotiate romance and non-organized marriage on their own.

My mother and father were roommates with three other people. This wasn't considered abnormal; many Tegaru lived in overcrowded boardinghouse-like settings to reduce expenses and maximize the money that could be sent back to Tigray to support their families. This was also made easier as the women worked as live-in maids, only leaving work one day a week. My mother was taken under the wing of an older woman who lived in the same house. It was considered unladylike to be in the company of a man unchaperoned, even in the late 1980s. When my mother finished work, she would wait for the woman to finish and they would go home together.

So, when my father kept pursuing my mom to date him? She refused and told him if he was serious to go ask her older male cousin in another town for her hand in marriage. In those times, it was considered loose to date. It could potentially "waste" your time and jeopardize your ability to make a good match as your name would be tarnished. Even worse would be to have a child out of wedlock. So, marriages were based on calculating risks and checking off a list: being a good provider from the same town in Tigray or nearby. My mom thought my dad was handsome and tall. The tall part was the clincher. She's five foot flat, but I am thankful for the dilution to her genetics, which has allowed me to grow to a whopping 5 feet 3 inches (160 cm).

The next day, my father bought a bus ticket to Gadarif to ask her cousin for her hand in marriage. Her cousin approved, but this was more a formality than an actual vetting. Her cousin said that he would give her away in place of her father. In our culture, when someone says they will give you away, it isn't the same as the Western definition of walking someone down the aisle, but rather saying a commitment to foot the bill and organize the wedding. It's a sign of honor and love for people to organize your wedding. Wedding planning is not in the hands of the couple, but their families.

She never got her big Tigray-style wedding. My father said they needed to rush as he had applied for sponsorship to go to the United States, and he wanted to submit the paperwork with her as his wife. As a result, she had a civil wedding and a small lunch gathering at her cousin's house. She later found out that the real reason my father had wanted to rush the wedding was because he had impregnated her roommate and wanted to walk my mom down the aisle before she found out. The woman he impregnated refused to say who the child's father was, initially.

> *The irony was that my mom visited her when she gave birth, as a newlywed, none the wiser about who the father was. Imagine the foolery!*

The woman was eventually required to disclose the child's father, as it is culturally important that a child is "claimed" and their lineage known to avoid communal shunning of some sort. A father claiming their existence is crucial for a child to be accepted into the community. My father was refusing to accept his child as he didn't want to jeopardize his new marriage, and extensive mediations took place as community members tried to convince him to do the right thing and claim his child. Community mediation (shmagle/ምሽምጋል) is an essential pillar of how all conflicts are addressed. A collective of respective community members will come and listen to both parties' grievances and make a determination that they deem fair. There is a lot of cultural pressure for people to attend mediation and accept the outcomes determined during the process. My mother wasn't privy to the mediation that was taking place.

There was an impasse in the process, as my father wasn't budging. A mutual friend said, "Let me tell his new wife, she is reasonable and she'll ask him to do the right thing." So, he came over when my dad was at work and told my mom the secret that the community had been pondering. She remembers exactly what she was doing at the time: she had just sat down to start cooking lunch. Her description of her emotions is directly translated as follows: "My head had split open and hot water was flowing out of it. I was frozen like a tree trunk."

When her guest left, she cried until she had a splitting headache. Her neighbor asked her what happened. She said her cousin had passed away. To cut a long story short, when she consulted her cousin about the issue he said something along the lines of "What's wrong with you? He is a man and that was before you got married." Basically, snap out of it. My father claimed his child. And this is how my parents commenced their marriage.

KEYIH SEBHI ቀይሕ ፀብሒ *Red lamb stew*

GF

Serves 4

Keyih sebhi directly translates as "red stew." This is a dish that is made for all celebratory occasions. You will never attend a wedding or a christening that doesn't serve this dish. It is traditionally made with lamb, goat, or beef. In Australia, we have even made it with kangaroo meat!

You can serve this dish on top of Injera (page 21) if you want to be traditional, or you can serve it on a bed of Ruz (page 64) or any rice. It goes perfectly with Ajebo (page 74) on the side.

INGREDIENTS

4 ripe tomatoes

6 garlic cloves, crushed

1 lb 12 oz (800 g) onions, finely diced

sunflower or vegetable oil, for cooking

7 oz (200 g) Dilik *(page 25)*

1 lb 12 oz (800 g) diced boneless goat

1 teaspoon salt

Ajebo *(page 74)***, to serve**

METHOD

Cook the tomatoes over an open flame on the stovetop using tongs until they start to char and blister (you can also do this under the broiler). When cool enough to handle, peel off the skins.

Put the tomatoes in a food processor with the crushed garlic and blend it to a paste.

Sauté the onion in sunflower oil in a heavy-based pot over low heat until translucent. You may need to stir to keep it from sticking.

Add the dilik to the pot and stir. If the mixture starts to stick, add just enough water to loosen it, but avoid flooding it, as you don't want to dilute the flavors. Keep cooking for about 10 minutes until the dilik and the onion look inseparable.

Add the tomato mixture to the pot and cook over low heat for another 10 minutes, adding more water as needed. The mixture should now be a burgundy color.

Add the meat and do your best to to coat it with the sauce base. You may need to add small amounts of water if the mixture starts to stick or the meat isn't quite submerged.

Let it cook for another 30–40 minutes, stirring regularly and ensuring you only add small quantities of water at a time. This is to ensure the flavor stays concentrated. Add the salt when you're about 5 minutes from taking it off the heat.

To check it's cooked, simply take out a piece of meat and check for tenderness.

ALJEBO ኣጅቦ *Cottage cheese*

GF V

Makes about 14 oz (400 g)

This is usually served in a similar way that yogurt is with Indian curries, as an accompaniment to spicy meat dishes such as Keyih sebhi (page 73).

INGREDIENTS

4¼ cups (1 liter) fresh whole milk

¼ cup (60 ml) freshly squeezed lemon juice

You will need a cheesecloth for this

METHOD

In a heavy-based pot, bring the milk to a gentle simmer. It should be foamy and steamy and read 185°F (85°C) on a thermometer.

Slowly pour in the lemon juice and stir until the milk separates and curds begin to form. This should take 5–7 minutes. Leave the heat on low.

Lay a piece of cheesecloth in a colander with a bowl underneath and pour the mixture on top. Set it aside until all the liquid has drained, then place the cheese in the fridge to chill. Serve cold.

This can last for a couple of days if sealed in an airtight container.

- You can also drink the whey, the liquid by-product of the cottage cheese.

AWAZE አዋዘ *Chile paste*

GF V VG

Makes about 5 cups (700 g)

An interesting delicacy Tegaru and Ethiopians enjoy is a spicy raw meat dish—steak tartare taken to another level. It is served at large celebrations, such as weddings, and at special eateries. The meat is very lean beef diced into small cubes and enjoyed with this chile paste and areki (ouzo).

INGREDIENTS

1 bulb of garlic, peeled

1 cup (175 g) hot mustard seeds

3⅔ cups (500 g) hot chile powder

3 tablespoons salt

METHOD

Put all the ingredients in a food processor and blend. The mixture should be like tomato sauce, but grainy. Add water as needed if the mixture is too dry.

This mixture will keep in an airtight container in the fridge for 3 months or so.

- You can also add this to plain Greek-style yogurt for a nice quick dip, or add it to mayonnaise-based salad dressings for a bit of a kick.

DEREK KULWA ደረቅ ቅልዋ

Beef rib and bell pepper stir-fry

GF

Serves 2

In Tigray there are special "meat houses." These are restaurants with butcheries attached that usually serve exclusively meat. You choose your cut and have it cooked for you. It is not customary that vegetables accompany the meat.

INGREDIENTS

sunflower oil, for cooking

14 oz (400 g) beef short ribs or back ribs (preferably with some of the fat left on) chopped into small chunks about ¾–1¼ inches (2–3 cm)

1 red onion, sliced

2 red bell peppers, chopped

2 green chiles, chopped

3 tablespoons Tesmi *(page 26)*

paprika

5 rosemary sprigs (whole)

Injera *(page 21)* **and Awaze** *(page 75)*, **to serve**

salt

METHOD

Heat some sunflower oil in a stockpot or heavy pot over medium heat and brown the beef, using tongs to turn it, then add some salt. The beef will start to release its fat; let it cook in the fat. Take the pot off the heat once all the liquid has evaporated.

Heat some more oil in a large frying pan over medium heat and sauté the onions, bell pepper, and chile for about 1 minute.

Add the tesmi, meat, and paprika to taste, and toss until brown. For the last minute of cooking add the rosemary sprigs, then remove.

Serve with injera and a side of awaze.

- You can pat your meat dry and sprinkle it with cornstarch and salt before cooking to ensure tenderness.

DULET ዱለት *Ground lamb tripe and liver*

GF

Serves 6

When I was a kid in Sudan I loved dulet! Then, when we moved to Australia and we had an indoor kitchen, no amount of ventilation could get rid of the smell of tripe and intestine for me not to couple the taste and smell.

The thing about delicacies is that they are very culturally specific. This dish is such a rarity, and is attached only to very special celebrations, as it is only enjoyed when a household butchers a whole beast. One can't get tripe and liver at a butcher in Tigray, and given one animal can only produce a limited amount of liver and tripe, it becomes truly special. At Christmas, Easter, or big holidays families will buy live animals and butcher them at home. One small issue is that most of the Orthodox religious holidays are preceded by an extensive vegan Lent, usually 40 days or more. It is also forbidden to participate in butchering during Lent, so families must wait for morning on the day they are breaking their Lent fast to butcher the animal. Men, usually of a certain age, do the butchering, preceded by a prayer. The women take all day to prepare the meals for the celebration. Usually dulet is made for breakfast, with the rest of the animal being cooked for lunch or dinner.

INGREDIENTS

14 oz (400 g) lamb tripe (see tip)

1 lb 9 oz (700 g) lamb liver

sunflower oil, for cooking

10½ oz (300 g) ground lamb

1 red onion, finely diced

5 garlic cloves, minced

3 tablespoons Dilik *(page 25)*

2 bunches of cilantro, leaves finely chopped

2–3 green chiles, finely diced (to your taste)

heaped 1 tablespoon Tesmi *(page 26)*, **or butter or lard**

Injera *(page 21)* **or flatbread, to serve**

salt

METHOD

Wash the tripe well, until there is no smell at all. Dice the tripe and liver as finely as possible. (It shouldn't stand out from the ground lamb too much.)

Put some sunflower oil in a frying pan and sauté the tripe for 5–6 minutes, stirring occasionally. Transfer to a bowl.

Add the ground lamb to the same pan and cook for 5–6 minutes, stirring occasionally. Transfer it to the bowl with the tripe.

Add the liver to the same pan and sauté for 5 minutes, stirring every few minutes. Transfer to the bowl.

In a large clean pan, heat some oil and sauté the onion until almost translucent, then add the garlic.

Add the dilik to the pan along with a little water if it begins to stick. Add the cilantro and green chile, stirring for 30 seconds before turning off the heat.

Add the tesmi and season with salt. Stir thoroughly, then transfer the contents of the bowl to the pan. Stir everything together until mixed well. Cook for 5 minutes over medium heat, ensuring you stir constantly.

Serve with injera or flatbread.

- Some butchers sell tripe well washed. I highly recommend you get that. This dish can be done with beef meat if need be. You can add intestines to this dish if you like!

KULWA BE MEREK ቅልዋ በ መረቅ

Beef stir-fry

GF

Serves 2

Although this is similar to Derek kulwa (page 77), the main difference is that it is a wetter consistency, giving you tasty juices.

INGREDIENTS

½ red onion, thinly sliced

sunflower oil, for cooking

14 oz (400 g) filet mignon, diced into ½ inch (1 cm) cubes

1 teaspoon vegetable bouillon powder, or mixed spices

½ teaspoon salt

1 teaspoon Dilik *(page 25)*, **or chile powder**

lukewarm water, for cooking

1 green or red chile, sliced

1 teaspoon Tesmi *(page 26)*, **or lard or butter**

Injera *(page 21)* **or flatbread, to serve**

METHOD

Put the onion and some sunflower oil in a frying pan over high heat. Sauté the onion for no more than 1 minute, stirring with a wooden spoon.

Add the steak to the pan and use the wooden spoon to move it around as you sear the meat for 1–2 minutes. The exterior of the meat should turn a brown color but not necessarily be cooked.

Turn the heat down to medium.

Add the stock powder, salt, and dilik and keep stirring.

If the meat starts to stick, add some lukewarm water—approximately ½ cup (125 ml). Reduce the heat to low. Cook until the spices have all mixed well. The liquid should take on the red color from the dilik and the smell of chile combined with the other flavors. This will take 2–3 minutes.

Add the chile and cook for another minute. Add the tesmi and mix well. As soon as the tesmi is incorporated, take the pan off the heat. Serve with injera or flatbread.

- Use splashes of water as you need to stop the ingredients sticking to the pan. You want to finish with a wet stir-fry texture.

QANTA ቋንጣ *Dried beef*

GF

Serves 4

*This is beef jerky Tigray style. Drying your own meat is common practice in Tigray. Given there is a propensity for families to butcher a full beast, the need for preservation becomes important. You would usually go into homes to find meat drying in open air on a string with light fabric over the top to prevent flies or dirt coming into contact with it. Once it's dried, they take what they need then make stews with it, such as Qanta fit fit (**page 85**) or snack on it as it is.*

INGREDIENTS

1 lb 2 oz (500 g) beef top round steak, or any other lean cut

2 teaspoons berbere spice mixture *(page 23)*, **or medium chile powder (not dilik)**

¼ teaspoon ground cardamom

¼ teaspoon ground black pepper

½ teaspoon salt

1 teaspoon vegetable oil

METHOD

Preheat the oven to 160°F (70°C).

Cut the meat into as thin strips as you possibly can to reduce the drying time. Pat it dry with paper towels, trying to remove as much excess liquid as possible. Place in a bowl.

Mix all the spices together with the oil and add to the bowl, then stir to coat all the meat evenly.

Place the strips evenly apart on an oven rack with a tray underneath to catch drips.

Let the strips dry in the oven for an hour, turning them at the 30 minute mark. From there, check on them every 30 minutes. The drying process can take 2–3 hours. How long it will take depends on the thickness of the strips and how much fat is on the meat.

They are ready when they start to stiffen, with cracks emerging and the strips bending. Store in an airtight container. Traditionally qanta is kept for months at room temperature.

- You can use a dehydrator if you have one.

QANTA FIT FIT ቋንጣ ፍትፍት

Dried beef stew with shredded injera

GF

Serves 2

This is similar to the Fit fit recipe (page 57), but uses dried meat.

INGREDIENTS

2 yellow onions, finely diced

sunflower oil, for cooking

2–3 garlic cloves, minced

heaped 1 tablespoon Dilik *(page 25)*

scant ½ cup (100 ml) hot water, plus extra as needed

scant 1 cup (180 g) diced tomatoes, (about 2 large tomatoes)

5¾ oz (160 g) Qanta *(page 82)*

½ tablespoon Tesmi *(page 26)*, **or butter or lard**

2 small or 1 large Injera *(page 21)*, **plus extra to serve**

green chiles, to serve

METHOD

In a pot over medium heat, sauté the onion in sunflower oil and stir until translucent. Add the minced garlic and cook for another minute.

Add the dilik and the hot water. Stir well, reduce the heat to low, and let it simmer for 15–20 minutes, adding small amounts of water each time it reduces so the onion doesn't burn.

(Here, you can choose to blend the tomatoes to a tomato paste consistency or leave them diced. The difference is if you don't mind the consistency of seeing little bits of tomato or if you would like the tomatoes to be blended into the stew.)

Add the tomato to the pot and let simmer for another 15 minutes.

Add the qanta and simmer for another 15 minutes. Add the tesmi and stir. After 2 minutes, turn off the heat.

Tear up the injera and stir well into the stew, to allow it to absorb the sauces. Scatter with chile and serve with more injera or bread on the side.

- If you don't want a chewy texture you can grind the qanta into a flour-like consistency.

HIS FAVORITE DISH WITH A SIDE OF MISTRESS

My parents had really different personalities. My father was about eight years older and more experienced in life, with reclusive tendencies, and was particular in how he liked things to be. My mother, at the time, was a naive country girl but was gregarious and social.

> *My father had a lucrative occupation as a professional fraudster. He would provide people with counterfeit passports and visas for them to be able to go to Europe from Khartoum.*

He was basically a people-smuggler via plane. I guess nineties travel technology was more rudimentary than today. Usually, the paperwork was legit, with an official having been paid off.

This afforded us a good lifestyle, relative to most Tegaru families in Khartoum. My mother didn't know or understand the details of what he did, merely that people came over and had hushed conversations, she served some tea or food and that was that. For context, this wasn't an occupation that was considered morally corrupt, but rather an essential service.

Tegaru in Khartoum were consistently in a transient headspace; they never put significant roots down.

The civil war ended in 1991, but they didn't have anything to go back to. The region was recovering from the devastation of a 17-year civil war, and too much had been lost. This, compounded by the fact that there were more job opportunities with better pay in Khartoum, led to Tegaru becoming significant financial supporters for their families in Tigray, and therefore made their geographic dislocation permanent. They became the necessary sacrificial lambs. Because

of this trend, there would be shame if they returned to Tigray without significantly changing their economic circumstances, so many lived in a state of limbo where they were always dreaming of returning home. They attempted to replicate home from fragments of their memories everywhere they went—that whole generation froze in time from the day that they left, holding onto this dream of returning home. But mostly, they never did; they just drifted further and further away.

They would say they'd return when they made "X" amount of money; then, as children were born in foreign countries, they would say when they finish high school, when they marry, and so on. As Tigray plunged into another war in November 2020, with more than 50,000 having fled in the first month, another generation will be geographically dislocated while the remainder keep dreaming of their return.

When I was two-and-a-half years old, there was a plan that my father would illegally migrate to Europe, settle in, and send for us. A week or two after he left, rumors began circulating that he had left with a pregnant mistress.

> ***My mother suspected an affair, but didn't know definitively. She was out running an errand one day and this elderly habesha woman started gossiping about my father to my mother.***

She said something along the lines of, "Did you hear about Mebrahtu? That prick left his young wife and kid for that whore. Poor woman, she is now stuck raising their child on her own." My mom feigned ignorance and simply said, "No I didn't hear." That is how she got her confirmation that my father had left us for another woman. He never officially separated or explained anything, but rather, she had a husband who left and became unreachable. He got in touch with my mom to say he had arrived safely and that was that until he reached out to me when I was 19 years old.

Ethiopians and Eritreans living in Khartoum always viewed themselves as in transit, some dreaming for a tomorrow in which they would return to the home they had fled. The stories of the past got grander and grander as time went by.

They would describe their five kilometer (three mile) country walk to school as a Jumanji *dystopia scene, the taste of honey straight from the hive surpassing galaxies, and family members left behind were immortalized in a way that made it seem like the whole state should be canonized. The truth was somewhere in between.*

The trauma of the unexpected separation didn't cease there; people kept coming to the house asking my mother to return the deposit that my father had taken promising forged papers that had never arrived.

People came into our house and tried to intimidate my mom into selling things, such as furniture, electronics, and jewelry, in order to pay them back. My mother had to quickly learn to stand up for herself and kick people out of the house with a retort like, "Did you give me the money?" These assets of my mother's would help sustain her and me over the years. As finances got tighter, she would sell an item here or there to supplement her income.

My mother never had a chance to process the separation, as she had to quickly go into survival mode. She had a toddler and a teenage niece who was boarding with us. She was the first in her family to have a "failed" marriage. I remember she wore her wedding band until I was nine years old. I used to always pester her about taking it off and she would just ignore me. Even as a child I remember thinking this was quite odd. We heard through the grapevine that my father had three more children and continued with the woman he left my mom for.

We have to be careful judging his actions, or the regular breakdown of families outside of the context they were raised in. These were people dislodged from their homes, their support system, coming of age during a civil war.

The impact of war and displacement doesn't stop when one gets to safety. It's cyclical and continues to have effects for generations.

FUL *Fava beans*

V

Serves 4

One of my father's favorite dishes was ful—a staple breakfast in Sudan. You can buy it ready-made at local corner shops or make it from scratch. There is a basic ful, or the gourmet variety where you add Tamia (falafel; page 93), feta, and even boiled eggs.

INGREDIENTS

2¾ cups (500 g) dried fava beans (broad beans), soaked overnight or until soft

olive oil, for cooking and serving

1 red onion, finely chopped

1 tomato, chopped, plus extra to serve

1 teaspoon ground cumin

4 hardboiled eggs, peeled and chopped

1 green chile, chopped, plus extra to serve

2¾ oz (80 g) Greek-style feta cheese, diced

Tamia *(page 93)*, **to serve**

toasted flatbread, to serve

Salata aswad *(page 92)*, **to serve**

salt

METHOD

Drain the fava beans and put them in a large pot. Cover with water, bring to a boil, and cook for 20–30 minutes.

Drain the beans and use a potato masher to smash them to a chunky consistency.

Put some olive oil into a frying pan over medium heat. Add the onion and stir until well cooked.

Add the tomato to the pan and cook for 1–2 minutes, then add the beans and stir.

Add the cumin and season with salt to taste, then cook for approximately 10 minutes.

Stir the boiled eggs into the mixture, add the green chile, then stir and turn off the heat.

Serve in a bowl, topped with feta, pieces of tamia, and extra tomato, plus a drizzle of olive oil. Serve alongside toasted bread of your choice and a bowl of salata aswad.

- You can make this dish vegan by omitting the egg and feta.

SALATA ASWAD *Eggplant dip*

GF V

Serves 4

This is a chunky eggplant dip that we usually would eat as a sandwich filling in Sudan. My mom used to give me this for school lunches.

INGREDIENTS

2 eggplants

sunflower or canola oil, for frying

½ cup (130 g) yogurt

3 tablespoons peanut butter

heaped 1 tablespoon olive oil, plus extra for drizzling

1 garlic clove, minced

½ teaspoon salt

1 green bell pepper, deseeded and finely diced

1 tomato, finely diced

juice of 1 lemon

gluten-free flatbread, to serve

METHOD

Peel and dice the eggplants into ½–¾ inch (1–2 cm) pieces.

Heat some oil in a frying pan over medium–high heat and add the diced eggplant.

Cook, stirring occasionally, for about 15 minutes until the eggplant softens. Set aside.

Mix together the yogurt, peanut butter, olive oil, garlic, and salt, until it's the consistency of mayonnaise. Set aside.

While it's lukewarm, put the eggplant in a food processor and pulse until it is the consistency of lumpy mashed potato.

Add the yogurt mixture and fold it through the eggplant mixture. Gently stir in the bell pepper, tomato, and the lemon juice.

Spread this on a toasted flatbread and drizzle with olive oil.

TAMIA *Falafel*

V VG

Makes 20

This is a little—approximately meatball-sized—snack made with chickpeas as the main ingredient.

INGREDIENTS

1½ cups (250 g) dried chickpeas, soaked overnight

2 onions

½ bulb of garlic, minced

3 green chiles, coarsely chopped

bunch of cilantro

1 cup (60 g) coarse breadcrumbs

2 teaspoons salt

peanut oil or sunflower oil, for frying

METHOD

Strain the chickpeas and put them in a food processor.

Peel and quarter the onions, then add them to the processor with the garlic, chile, cilantro, breadcrumbs, and salt. Blend to a smooth, thick consistency.

Take out the mixture and form into 1¼ inch (3 cm) balls. Slightly flatten them out.

Heat a deep frying pan with about 1 inch (2.5 cm) of oil over medium heat. Place the tamia in the pan, working in batches if necessary, and cook for 3 minutes, turning them over halfway through. Remove from the pan when they become a dark brown color. Place on paper towels to drain the excess oil.

These are usually served as an accompaniment to Ful (page 91), but also as fillings for bread rolls.

- You can store the mixture in the freezer for future use. It can last for months. Simply defrost before use. If the mixture dries out too much you can use a bit of oil or water to reintroduce moisture. Use gluten-free breadcrumbs to make this gluten-free.

Pregnancy cravings

Traditionally, pregnancy is a private affair not discussed until it is noticeable, not even with the baby's father. It's even considered premature to speak of your pregnancy in your first trimester, given the risk of miscarriage.

Women usually continue with their daily duties with a strong belief that keeping active will quicken the labor. If it's a woman's first child, she will go home to her family in the eighth month to relax and prepare for the birth. The husband will remain in their marital home. She will have a baby shower, called Ga'at (like the food), where women come around to eat, sing birthing songs, and dance. The songs are centered around a safe delivery and asking for Virgin Mary to protect the soon-to-be mother. They do not buy any clothing for the baby before the birth as it's considered bad luck.

My mother found out early in her pregnancy that she would be having a caesarean section with me, as my head was too large, or her hips too small. This wasn't a common occurrence in 1989 in Khartoum, and she was even asked to find people of the same blood type to donate blood just in case she lost too much during the surgery. That's right: my parents had to go out and find people with the same blood type to donate in anticipation for a potential heavy blood loss. I guess this takes BYO to a new level.

When my mother was pregnant, my grandmother lived on the farm in Adi Kuhla about a one-and-a-half hour walk from Aksum. My mother asked my grandma to come and help her during her recovery. My grandmother, who had never left Tigray and was a devout Orthodox woman, could not cope with the idea of going to a country that was Muslim. Sudan did and still does run on Sharia law, so she told my mother, "May Virgin Mary be with you as I can't step into a Muslim country." That was a bitter disappointment for my mother to miss the experience of having her mother there for the birth of her first child. My mother was deeply saddened not to have the ritual of retreating to her mother's in her eighth month of pregnancy, or have her stay with her to recover. My grandmother had been there for the birth of most of her grandchildren.

SEMEK *Fried tilapia*

Serves 4

This is usually served with a salad and some bread.

INGREDIENTS

6 garlic cloves, crushed

1 teaspoon ground cumin

½ teaspoon freshly ground black pepper

1½ teaspoons salt

juice of 1 lemon

4 tilapia fillets (about 7 oz/200 g each)

1 cup (150 g) all-purpose flour

sunflower oil, for deep-frying

Timatim salata *(page 98)***, lemon wedges, and sliced green chile, to serve**

METHOD

Combine the garlic, cumin, pepper, and ½ teaspoon of the salt in a bowl and mix well. Mix in the lemon juice.

Add the fish fillets to the bowl and turn to coat evenly. Cover and leave to marinate for 30 minutes.

Mix the flour and the remaining salt and spread it on a flat tray or plate.

Heat the oil for deep-frying in a frying pan (Shallow-frying is also an option.)

Coat the fish in a thin layer of flour and place in the oil. If shallow-frying, cook for 2 minutes on each side. If deep-frying, cook until it's brown.

Put paper towels on a plate and lay the fillets on top to drain any excess oil.

Serve with the timatim salata, some lemon wedges, and sliced green chile.

TIMATIM SALATA *Tomato salad*

GF V

Serves 2

This salad is usually an accompaniment to meat dishes, but it also tastes delicious as a filling for fresh bread.

INGREDIENTS

SALAD

4 tomatoes

⅔ cup (100 g) Greek-style feta cheese (crumbled or chopped into ½ inch/1 cm cubes)

¼ red onion, finely chopped

1 green chile, deseeded and finely chopped

DRESSING

1 teaspoon olive oil

1 teaspoon white vinegar

1 teaspoon freshly squeezed lemon juice

½ teaspoon salt

METHOD

Dice the tomatoes into ½ inch (1 cm) pieces. Mix with the remaining salad ingredients.

Mix the dressing separately and toss through the salad.

KEYSIR SALATA ቀይሕ ስር ሳላጣ

Beet and bacon salad

GF

Now, let's talk about Tigray cuisine and pig products. My brethren probably saw the bacon as an ingredient and were ready to meet me on Twitter, so let me explain ... The bacon is purely an addition I enjoy rather than a part of the original recipe. Tegaru—yes, all—traditionally do not eat pig products for religious reasons, both in Orthodox Christianity and Islam. Those of other denominations tend to make up less than 0.05 percent of the population and, for them, culture influences their dining choices. The fact that Muslims don't eat it might not be surprising, but let's explain why Orthodox Christians don't. This is based on the Old Testament that talks about suitability of animals for consumption. For mammals to be served as a food they need to be ruminants with split hooves and birds must have fully split fingers. According to this religious belief, therefore, pig doesn't fulfill the criteria. However, other Orthodox Christian followers, for example Greeks and Russians, have allowed the consumption of pig products.

To my mother's dismay, let's just say my sister and I developed a taste for salami, ham, and bacon. She was liberal enough to buy it for us, but wouldn't cook with it. This transgression did not warrant us being shipped off to Tigray. ›

KEYSIR SALATA ቀይሕ ስር ሳላጣ

Beet and bacon salad

GF

Serves 2

INGREDIENTS

SALAD

2 potatoes (any kind)

2 beets

1 green chile, core removed, sliced

½ red onion, diced

½ cup (75 g) fried and diced bacon rashers (optional; see intro)

DRESSING

3 tablespoons olive oil

1 teaspoon salt

heaped 1 tablespoon freshly squeezed lemon juice

1 teaspoon English mustard (my mother prefers the spicy nature of this, but you can leave it out if you like)

METHOD

Put the potatoes and beets in a large pot full of water and bring to a boil. The beets should take approximately 30 minutes and the potatoes about 10 minutes. Simply check this by pricking with a fork. Avoid overcooking, as it will be too mushy.

Once the beets and potatoes have been taken off the stove and have cooled down, peel them. Then dice them to your desired size.

Mix all the dressing ingredients in a bowl.

In a salad bowl, mix the beets, potatoes, chile, onion, and bacon. Mix the dressing into the salad evenly and enjoy. This salad is typically served as an accompaniment to legume stews such as Birsen *(page 115)*.

MAY VIRGIN MARY BE WITH YOU

Childbirthing is very much women's business in Tigray, with men traditionally having very little to do with the babies until they reach toddler age. Although there have been slight cultural shifts recently, they haven't been too significant.

In the labor room, a woman would have her mother (or a female relative) and a midwife. If labor lasts longer than a day, gunshots may be fired to induce birth by shock. Although this is an obscure practice, there is medical research that stress can induce labor.

After the umbilical cord was cut, it would be tied to the woman's leg to prevent the cord and placenta slipping back into her uterus. Once a woman gives birth, the midwife massages the woman's abdomen with butter to accelerate the delivery of the placenta. If it's considered partially discharged, the midwife will press a water jar down on the abdomen until all the remnants are discharged.

Women in the new mother's life will come to "alae'la"—basically, take over all her domestic duties and take care of any other children she may have. For the first seven days the new mother doesn't leave the home. She is brought food and drinks to give the her time to attach to her baby and recover from labor.

On day seven, the women will put hair butter in her hair or braid it and she will step over a coal fire. She is taken to the front yard, or equivalent, to bask in the sun while they make coffee for her. The baby is sunbaked for the first time on both sides. There will be singing and dancing to celebrate the birth, and it is a strictly women-only affair, of course. From here on, the mother will take her baby out every morning to sunbathe in the early morning sun. The significance of this custom isn't explained in detail, but it signifies that the mother can now leave her birthing room. There is a forced intense recovery and bonding that takes place for the seven days after giving birth. After this time, the new mother is reintroduced to the outside world.

> ***The seventh day is also when they strap a waist cincher around her waist to help snap her abdomen area back into shape. She usually won't return to full duties until after the christening.***

Male babies get circumcized quite early on, at less than two weeks old. It is recommended they get circumcized before they start rolling or moving their legs in order to help with recovery. The baby boy is also expected to have recovered in time for his christening.

The concept of "postpartum depression" is unknown within the Tigray culture. Initially, I had attributed that to the culture not being expressive, but it might be the result of new mothers being given so much support and space to bond with their child without the stress of partaking in all the other household duties. There aren't pressures on the mother beyond attending to her child, and she has around-the-clock support as she undertakes this role at least until the baby's christening.

> ***Children are christened at 40 days for boys and at 80 days for girls, with their hair shaved. They are given a church name, usually after the saint's day of their christening, and are given a single godparent of the same gender. Godparents are charged with being their spiritual mentors.***

My grandmother was a midwife and undertaker—she bringeth and taketh away. It was a practice that was taught to her by her mother, but she wasn't able to pass it on to her daughters, as they were squeamish. She was absolutely disappointed that upon her death someone outside of the family would have to see her potentially defecating herself. To her, that was dishonorable—even in death—that someone outside of your family might see what is natural biology. Tegaru can sometimes take respectability too far.

During my grandmother's generation—and among current regional women—birth control wasn't used and people had as many kids as they could birth. Usually, the children were spaced two or three years apart and child mortality was quite high. If there is a toddler in the house, the father won't hold the infant to prevent the toddler being jealous and wanting to harm the baby.

> *The father becomes the main parent for the toddler and the mother for the infant. My grandmother birthed 12 children. Only nine survived to adulthood. She was giving birth to my mother while simultaneously becoming a grandmother.*

GA'AT ጋዓት *Tigray-style gnocchi*

V

Serves 4

This is a dish that is made for new mothers and any guests who come to visit for almost the first month after having a child.

INGREDIENTS

2½ cups (300 g) all-purpose flour

1 teaspoon salt

4 tablespoons melted Tesmi *(page 26)*

heaped 1 tablespoon Dilik *(page 25)*

¾ cup (200 g) Greek-style yogurt

METHOD

Toast the flour in a dry nonstick frying pan over medium heat, stirring constantly using a wooden spoon. Toast for about 2 minutes, or until it browns to an almond color. Sift the flour and set aside.

In a pot with an extended handle, put 3 cups (750 ml) water and the salt and bring to a boil. Also boil a kettle of water separately and set aside.

Get a large serving bowl and coat it with 1 tablespoon of tesmi and set aside for later.

Slowly add the flour to the water while stirring with a wooden spoon (not a whisk). Try to add ½ cup (125 ml) at a time to achieve a smooth mixture. You want to reach a pizza-dough consistency—soft and slightly sticky, but not wet. As you add more flour it will be harder to mix and become laborious on your arms. If you find there is flour not mixed in, add very small amounts of water from the kettle you had set aside, being careful not to add too much at once.

Once you have achieved the desired consistency, remove the ga'at from the heat and transfer it to your serving bowl. Use the wooden spoon to sculpt it into one big ball.

In the center of the ball, make a well using a stainless steel spoon. Mix the remaining tesmi and the dilik together while the ga'at is still hot and place it in the well you've created. Spoon the yogurt into the bowl, around the edges of the dough.

The way to eat this is with your fingers (or a fork). Pinch a piece of dough the size of a single mouthful, then dip it into the middle of the tesmi-dilik sauce and scoop a bit of the yogurt for each mouthful.

SHIPPED OFF AT FOUR YEARS OLD FOR PRAYING TO THE WRONG GOD

Sudan operated on Sharia law—the government, Islamic faith, and law being inseparable. Sharia law created cultural clashes along faith lines at times for Tegaru, most of whom are Orthodox Christians (about 95 percent of the population).

Khartoum had layers of class division: foreigners working for non-governmental organizations, Middle Eastern/Arab businessmen, North Sudanese, Habesha folks (Eritreans/Ethiopians/Tegaru) and, at the bottom of the totem pole, South Sudanese and Falatas (descendants of Nigerian migrants from previous centuries). This class difference was exacerbated by differences of faith. There wasn't much social interaction between the different groups.

> *This created anxiety among Orthodox Tegaru about losing their kids to the dominant culture or faith.*

Tegaru, prior to this civil war, did not migrate in significant numbers, nor did they have many migrants come into the state. People were born, married, and died in the same region, having not come across anyone too different from them.

> *Khartoum had a generation of first migrants who were having children in transient cities they never expected to stay in, without extended family and with children speaking Arabic as their first language and converting to Islam.*

My mother, as a priest's daughter and generally operating at a higher level of anxiety, was petrified of this possible outcome. As a result, my first language was Tigrinya, my mom exclusively talked Tigrinya in the house, and insisted all visitors comply with this rule. I grew up among the community of Tegaru going to concerts and fundraisers.

When I was four years old my mom enrolled me in a primary school. She said, "You talked too much and never napped, so may as well go to school." She also needed the childcare school would offer so she could work uninterrupted as a street vendor at the front of our house.

She took me to a Sudanese primary school, saying I was turning five soon even though I had 10 months to go. They weren't too fussy with birth certificate checks and all that.

In Sudan, Islam is intricately woven into everyday society, making it impossible to unpick. So, at school during the Salah (five prayers practiced by Muslims) times, all the kids would line up and we would pray. The teachers knew I was Orthodox but there wasn't much respect for faith variations, I guess, so they taught me to pray.

One day I came home and heard the call to prayer from the local mosque. I assumed the position and started praying. My mom was absolutely shocked and told me, "Don't you dare do that! We are not Muslims, we are Christians."

I went to school the next day and when the call to prayer came, I told my teachers, "I am not praying, I am Christian."

After that day I felt excluded, so I came home and said, "People don't like me the same way anymore. You either take me out of this school or I am praying with them." Yes, that's what I said to my mom at four years old.

This experience for my mother was terrifying. By this point, she was a single mother and didn't want to lose her only child to a culture that she felt was alien to her.

She took me out of the school and, given there were no alternatives at that time, she decided to send me to live with her family in Tigray.

My mom took me to Tigray to meet my family for the first time and for me to live with one of my aunts in Aksum. Well, I was a fussy eater and my mom had to feed me with a wooden spoon, so my aunt said no, take her to Addis, "I am scared she will be dead here." So, my mom took me to my aunt's in Addis Ababa. I turned five years old soon after arriving in Addis. I was told that we had come to visit the family. I had no idea I was supposed to be living there.

All I knew was I woke up one morning and my mama was gone. No hoo-ha, no fuss, no tears. My aunt told me some vague story that my mom was going to the Middle East to work as a maid and that's why she left me there. Many Tegaru women did leave Sudan to work in the Middle East as live-in maids and nannies, as they would make more money. Taking their kids wasn't an option, so they would leave their kids with family. That's the irony: they raise other women's kids while someone else raises theirs.

> *I just knew, even at the tender age of five, there wasn't room for me to fuss—it just was. I wished every day she would come back, not because my aunt mistreated me or anything. But because I was struggling with the lifestyle and cultural change.*

I went from being the only child with so many pseudo-aunts and uncles who were childless and spoiled me, to being one of three kids in the house. Khartoum also had better living standards than Addis in the nineties. For a kid, that translated to access to cookies, soft drinks, and lollipops at a much higher rate. It was a very tight community in Khartoum; people didn't have their families, so the community was their family.

As a child, I happily belonged to the collective. In Addis, people had their immediate and extended family around so they didn't have the need to overextend themselves to others.

> *For the two years I was there, all I remember is eating birsen almost daily until my mom came back to get me. Surprisingly, it's now my favorite dish that my mom makes!*

It had not been easy for my mom to return. Even though there was no war at that time and the country was relatively stable, those who had left during the war found themselves economically and culturally shut out. Their families were better off financially with them away. And they were able to work and send back essential funds to their families from Sudan. Culturally, there was a sense towards those who left that they hadn't suffered like those who had stayed. My mom talks about feeling ashamed to go back without having financially "made it," or having done something that matters. This was a major hurdle when she considered returning home from Australia as well. But I was glad she did.

In the next section of this book there will be predominantly vegan dishes. It's important to note that while these recipes have serving sizes that assume you may only make one dish at a time, this is usually not the way Tegaru prefer to eat unless financial circumstances dictate it. Usually, mothers will make multiple vegetarian dishes to be eaten at the same time—think of it like yum cha. A little bit of this and a little bit of that.

> *Until this day, I struggle to commit to choosing one dish at a restaurant and insist that dinner companions share their food with me to give me variety.*

BIRSEN ብርስን *Split red lentil curry*

GF V VG

Serves 4

This is a very popular dish, particularly during Lent. It is a curry enjoyed with injera. The consistency can also lend itself to being eaten as a soup.

INGREDIENTS

1 cup (200 g) split red lentils

1 onion, finely diced

sunflower oil, for cooking

heaped 1 tablespoon finely chopped garlic

heaped 1 tablespoon Dilik *(page 25)*

1 ripe tomato

1 teaspoon salt

Injera *(page 21)* **or rice, to serve**

METHOD

Wash the lentils until the water runs clear. This may take four or five washes. According to my mother, shortcutting this process will give you indigestion and create discomfort in your stomach. It also leaves the lentils with an earthy flavor that you don't want.

In a pot over medium heat, sauté the onion in just enough oil to stop it sticking. When the onion starts to brown, add the garlic and sauté for another minute or so, then add the dilik.

Meanwhile, flame-grill the tomato directly over an open flame on the stove, turning as necessary. (You can also do this under the broiler.) Once the skin starts to blacken a little, take it off the flame and peel it with your fingers. Chop coarsely and blend in a food processor until you have a paste-like consistency.

Add the processed tomato to the onion mix.

Add the lentils and 3 cups (750 ml) of water to the pot and cook for 15–25 minutes. If it's too thick but still not cooked, you can add a bit more water.

Add the salt and stir. When it's complete, the lentils should have expanded and taste tender. Serve with injera or rice.

DEFUN BIRSEN ድፋን ብርሰን

Green lentil stew

GF V VG

Serves 4

This is another staple during Lent.

INGREDIENTS

1 cup (200 g) green lentils

1 onion, diced

sunflower oil, for cooking

2 garlic cloves, minced

1 teaspoon ground turmeric

1 teaspoon ground cumin

2 teaspoons salt, or to taste

Injera *(page 21)*, **Hamli** *(page 120)*, **and Dinish** *(page 127)*, **to serve**

METHOD

Wash the lentils until the water runs clear, then drain and leave to the side.

In a pot, sauté the onion in oil over medium heat until translucent. Add the garlic, turmeric, and cumin to the pot and stir well. Cook for 5 minutes, adding just a splash of water to get a thick paste.

Add the lentils to the pot with 1⅔ cups (400 ml) of water and reduce the heat to low. Ensure the lentils are submerged by at least 2 inches (5 cm) of water.

Stir the lentils, put the lid on, and cook for 20 minutes, stirring every 5 minutes or so. Add the salt to the pot and cook for another 5 minutes. You want the lentils to keep their round shape and puff up.

Serve this on injera, and with hamli and dinish as accompaniments.

ALICHA BIRSEN አሊጫ ብርስን

Yellow split pea stew

GF V VG

Serves 4

This is another Lent staple. It also tends to be popular with people who don't eat spicy food—although in Tegaru communities, those are few and far between.

INGREDIENTS

scant 1 cup (200 g) yellow split peas

1 onion, finely diced

sunflower oil, for cooking

2 garlic cloves, minced

1 teaspoon ground turmeric

½ teaspoon cumin

2 teaspoons salt, or to taste

Injera *(page 21)*, **to serve**

METHOD

Wash the yellow split peas until the water runs clear, then drain and leave to the side.

In a pot, sauté the onion in a little oil over medium heat until translucent.

Add the garlic and turmeric to the pot and stir well. Cook for 5 minutes, adding just a tad of water to get a thick paste.

Add the lentils to the pot with 1⅔ cups (400 ml) of water and reduce the heat to low.

Ensure the lentils are submerged by at least 2 inches (5 cm) of water. Add the cumin.

Stir the lentils, place the lid on, and let them cook for 20 minutes, stirring every 5 minutes or so. Add the salt and cook for another 5 minutes. The stew will get thicker and the split peas will lose their shape, looking like full rather than half-circles.

Serve this on injera.

HAMLI ሓምሊ *Sautéed greens*

GF V VG

Serves 2

This is a winter staple in Tigray. Hamli grows wild all over the countryside come winter time, making this a great food for subsistence farmers waiting on the spring harvest. This weed-like plant is known as Chinese broccoli or gai lan in many countries and may cost you a mint per bundle (see tip). This dish is best served with legume stew as a complement.

INGREDIENTS

2 bundles of Chinese broccoli (gai lan)

½ onion, finely chopped

sunflower oil, for cooking

4 garlic cloves, finely chopped

1 whole green chile *(see tip)*

salt

METHOD

Wash the Chinese broccoli and chop off the stalk ends. Finely dice the stalks and shred the leaves. Keep the stalks and leaves separate.

Sauté the onion in some oil in a large pot over medium heat, then add the garlic.

Once softened, add the stalks. Once the stalks start to soften, add the leaves.

Trim the stalk off the green chile, cut it down the center to reveal the seeds, and throw it into the dish. Cook until the greens are soft, season with salt, and serve with a protein of your choice.

- The green chile will not make it spicy, but will give it an aromatic flavor. You can choose to cook the onion in Tesmi (page 26) if you want a more decadent flavor. You can replace the Chinese broccoli with Swiss chard.

ENTATIE SEBHI እንጣጢዕ ፀብሒ *Flaxseed stew/dip*

GF V VG

Serves 2

This dish is another pauper person's friend. The consistency of it is more like a dip than a stew, but it is typically eaten like a stew. It is often served to people with an upset stomach. You can find flaxseed (linseed) in the health food aisle at the supermarket, or at healthfood stores.

INGREDIENTS

¾ cup (100 g) flaxseeds (linseed)

1 onion, finely chopped

1 teaspoon ground garlic

sunflower oil, for cooking

1 teaspoon Dilik *(page 25)*

2 cups (500 ml) hot water (not boiling, but warmer than lukewarm)

Injera *(page 21)*, **to serve**

METHOD

Toast the flaxseed for 2 minutes in a dry frying pan. This can get messy, as the seeds have a tendency to jump out of the pan.

Transfer to a tray and set aside to cool for 10–15 minutes. Grind the toasted seeds into a granulated texture and put aside.

Sauté the onion and garlic in oil in a small saucepan, and add the dilik.

Let it simmer for 5–10 minutes, then add the ground flaxseed to the pot, whisking and adding 1¼ cups (300 ml) of the hot water until it's a smooth consistency.

Add another ⅔ cup (170 ml) of hot water and keep whisking. You may need the extra water if the flaxseed isn't mixing well. Let it simmer for 20–25 minutes over low heat.

This is usually served with injera. You can try shredding the injera into pieces and pouring the entatie sauce all over it.

DINISH ዱንሽ

Potato, cabbage, and carrot stew

GF V VG

Serves 4

This will be a great replacement for your average potato salad, or maybe even a steak and dinish dinner could be on the cards for you. Usually this is served as part of a vegan platter and it is sometimes the first solid food babies are started on.

INGREDIENTS

2 onions, finely diced

oil, for cooking (any oil without a strong taste is fine)

heaped 1 tablespoon finely chopped fresh garlic

heaped 1 tablespoon ground turmeric

2 carrots, peeled and sliced

5 potatoes (about 2 lb 10 oz/1.2 kg), peeled and diced

½ head green cabbage, shredded

1 teaspoon salt, or to taste

2 green chiles

METHOD

Sauté the onion in a pot with just enough oil to stop it sticking. When the onion starts to brown, add the garlic and sauté for another minute or so.

Add the turmeric and stir, then add a bit of water so the mixture looks like paste.

Add the carrots and cook for 5–10 minutes until they are al dente. Add the potatoes, and cook for another 5 minutes, stirring throughout to ensure even cooking.

Add the shredded cabbage, salt, and the whole green chiles. Cook until the cabbage starts to wilt.

It will continue to cook once you take it off the stove. Be careful not to overcook the potatoes, as you will end up with mash instead of dinish.

DUBA ዱባ *Pumpkin stew*

GF V VG

Serves 4

Because of the chunky nature of this stew, people often prefer to have it as an accompaniment to one of the legume stews.

INGREDIENTS

3 ripe tomatoes

1 teaspoon ground cumin

4 onions, finely diced

sunflower oil, for cooking

7 garlic cloves, minced

4 tablespoons Dilik or berbere spice mixture *(pages 23–25)*

½ butternut squash or pumpkin, peeled and diced into 2 inch (5 cm) cubes

2 teaspoons salt, or to taste

Injera *(page 21)*, **to serve**

METHOD

Cook the tomatoes over an open flame on the stovetop using tongs until they start to blacken (you can also do this under the broiler). When cool enough to handle, peel off the skins.

Blend the tomatoes and cumin in a food processor and set aside.

Sauté the onion in oil in a pot over medium heat until translucent. Add the garlic and sauté for 1 minute. Add the dilik and cook for another minute. (If you are using berbere spice mixture, add a little bit of water to create a paste-like consistency.)

Add the processed tomatoes to the pot and cook for about 5 minutes before adding the squash, tossing to ensure it's well coated. Add enough water to submerge the squash and cook until tender. You should be able to gauge this by seeing if you can use a fork to break a piece up.

Serve with injera.

- It can be easy to overcook the squash, as the dish will continue to cook in the residual heat of the pot.

KEYSIR ቀይሕ ስር

Beet stew

GF V VG

Serves 2

This dish is not very common in rural areas and tends to be more of an urban dish.

INGREDIENTS

½ onion, finely diced

oil, for cooking (any oil without a strong flavor is fine)

1 teaspoon finely chopped fresh garlic

4 beets, peeled and cut into cubes (about ½ inch/1 cm)

½ teaspoon salt, or to taste

METHOD

Sauté the onion in a sauté pan over medium heat with just enough oil to stop it sticking. When the onion starts to brown, add the garlic and sauté for another minute or so.

Add the beets and salt and cook for 5–10 minutes until al dente.

STARVIN' MARVIN

I wasn't yet born during the 1984 famine that gripped the northern regions of Ethiopia, predominantly affecting modern-day Tigray. My mother had left only a few months before it had reached her town. This was a famine estimated to have killed up to one million people.

The first time I heard of this famine was when I was in primary school in Australia (circa 2000) when a kid on the playground started calling me "Starvin' Marvin." I didn't quite get the reference. The taunting didn't stop there, either—it was followed by jokes along the lines of, "How do you make an Ethiopian run? Dangle a slice of bread in front of them." This was the height of comedy in my school playground. This shame would follow me home as popular TV shows everyone at school watched were filled with World Vision ads focusing on Ethiopia. People I hadn't met yet would say, "Like the World Vision ad," as they baited me with the "Where are you really from?" question.

Ethiopia experiences periodic famines, with Tigray disproportionately affected due to various ecological factors: drought, lack of modernized agricultural systems, and animal and plant disease. This vulnerability has been exacerbated and famine weaponized over generations to oppress and make the people of Tigray yield.

> ***Tegaru have consistently revolted against the Ethiopian state's ethnic persecution, since power of the throne shifted from the north to Shewa in the mid-nineteenth century.***

The first significant rebellion in Tigray began in 1941, called First Woyane, meaning "revolutionary." A group of rebels formed from the semi-pastoralists of Raya Azebo: some local feudal lords and disgruntled peasants, under the military leadership of Hailemariam Reda, nearly succeeded in overrunning the whole province. Addis invited the British Royal Air Force to bomb the region in 1943. Throughout this period, the Federal Government weakened the rebellion further by interrupting the salt trade, confiscating cattle, and engaging in the looting of farms.

> *In 1971–1973 there was a crop failure in Tigray during Haile Selassie's reign. Addis was more preoccupied about hiding the situation than providing any substantial support to the region.*

The Emperor was accused of having spent over US $30 million on celebrating his 80th birthday and infamous images of pampered royal dogs circulated while people in the north were dying of starvation. Grains were imported from India, but none were distributed to the northern regions, with most going to Addis only. This contributed greatly to the demise of the last Emperor and led to the successful coup that saw the Marxist–Leninist Derg regime come into power.

Another famine gripped the northern regions during the Derg regime in the 1980s. Addis again exacerbated periodic agricultural failures in Tigray. In 1983, the government launched a two-front campaign in Tigray, from Eritrea and Wollo, to quell the unrest that was brewing in the populace. The campaign was aimed against Eritrean secession forces and the broader unrest that was brewing across Tigray. They bombed schools, markets, and villages, destroyed grain stores, burned farms, and displaced farmers with the support of the Soviet Union arms trade. The Soviet Union gave the Derg regime military aid following the Ogaden War.

Derg's land reform policies seriously distressed Tigray's farmers, who had suffered badly organized and unfair land redistribution, new taxes, and the forced sale of produce at below market price. Moreover, farmers' households' economies were jeopardized by the prohibition of working in towns and hiring agricultural laborers. This was an essential element of the Tigray economy.

Derg attempted to starve peasants out of their commitment to the fighters by interfering with food production, sales, and delivery. There was an attempt to cover up this famine, forcing liberation fighters (TPLF) to walk thousands of starving Tegaru to Sudan to highlight what was happening. This famine did affect Addis as well, as residents struggled to pay inflated grain prices. However, the impact was disproportionately devastating in the northern regions.

> *This was compounded by the fact that the Derg regime aligned itself with the Soviet Union, which at the time had limited grain reserves with the US, with the European Economic Community having the bulk. The ideological battlefield—the Cold War—had a direct impact on Ethiopian politics and food security in Tigray.*

The Derg regime had dedicated more than 60 percent of its resources to state farms and collectivized producers' cooperatives that yielded less than the previous set up, along with pursuing land reform policies and fighting continued unrest with TPLF (Second Woyane). In June–July 1984, the rains again failed, with places like Wollo, Sidamo, Harerghe, Gondar, Shewa, and Tigray suffering the worst of it. The Federal Government and state media did not cover what was going on, despite the famine beginning to affect the Capital with inflated food prices.

The Derg government was unwilling to divert resources, attention, and money from the 10-year anniversary of coming into office, four-day celebrations that would commence in September 1984—with dignitaries from Eastern Bloc countries being invited to see all the commotion. In October of that year, two BBC television reporters were somehow granted access to internally displaced people camps in Tigray. This gave us Bob Geldof's "Do They Know It's Christmas?"

Throughout this period, the unrest in the Tigray region continued, and was further fueled by the sense of injustice about how the famine was mismanaged. (Meanwhile, there was also a strong secession movement from Eritrean forces, given they had been annexed by Ethiopia following a United Nations resolution in 1952, which ignored the independence sentiment from the populace. After decades of liberation movements, Eritrea eventually gained its independence in 1993.)

The repeated use of starvation and famine to bring Tegaru in line has been seen again in the declaration of war that happened on November 4th, 2020, under the guise of Law and Order under the leadership of Prime Minister Abiy Ahmed.

There was no drought or harvest failure that led to the recent and ongoing mass starvation. Ethiopian forces and Eritrean allies have engaged in heavy bombardment of food-grain storage, the looting or killing of cattle, and in scorched-earth tactics, burning farms as troops move through. All of these devastating tactics have combined with the already brutal economic effects of living in a war zone. The United Nations estimated in April 2021 that 91 percent of the Tigray population needs emergency food aid, with the Federal Government still prohibiting humanitarian access. Aid organizations have only been allowed to enter the region intermittently even a year after the conflict started, and more than 20 aid workers have been killed.

> *In other words, famine in Tigray is not inherent—rather, it has been caused by political apathy and the deliberate weaponization of hunger to control the region.*

KINTISHARA SEBHI ቁንቲሻራ

Sautéed mushrooms

GF V VG

Serves 2

When I had been in Australia for long enough to start asking Mom to buy things I hadn't seen before, I asked her to buy some mushrooms because I had eaten them on a pizza and wanted to try them at home. My mom couldn't understand the appeal of a weed that grows wild and people eat when they have nothing else and the crops have failed. The concept of paying for mushrooms continues to amuse her.

INGREDIENTS

3 ripe tomatoes

5 garlic cloves, peeled and crushed

2 onions, finely diced

sunflower oil, for cooking

3 tablespoons Dilik *(page 25)*

1 lb 6 oz (640 g) sliced mushrooms

Injera *(page 21)*, **to serve**

salt

METHOD

Sear the tomatoes over an open flame on the stovetop using tongs until they start to blacken (you can also do this under the broiler). When cool enough to handle, peel off the skins.

Blend the tomatoes in a food processor with the crushed garlic and set aside.

Put the onion in a pot with some oil and fry over medium heat until translucent.

Add the dilik and cook until mixed well with the onions.

Add the processed tomato and cook over low heat for about 15 minutes until you have a dark crimson color. Season with salt to taste.

Add the mushrooms to the pot and cook for 5 minutes. When ready, the sauce should be reduced and thickened to a stew, similar to a chunky bolognese sauce.

Serve with injera.

LEAVING SUDAN

My mother and I migrated to Melbourne from Sudan in 1999. Tegaru migrated to Australia from Khartoum through two different systems: organization sponsorship (e.g. Red Cross), or through Tegaru who had migrated previously—the latter is more likely. Your sponsors would send you a form to say that they will pay for all your expenses until you settle in, pay for your medical assessments before arrival, flights, and so on. We had to get tested for various diseases and get vaccinations. You could fail a medical examination and be denied your visa.

As I was growing up in Melbourne, Anglo–Australians were always fascinated by how we ended up here—even down to the visa category—"Did you come here as a refugee?" They would ask in a high-pitched quizzical voice, listening intently so they could retell your migration journey at their next dinner gathering. I'm being slightly tongue-in-cheek, but I would be fibbing if I didn't say there was at least a tablespoon of truth in it.

> *This question for new migrants feels as intrusive as asking someone what their tax bracket is.*

Why? Because our stories are complex and cannot fit neatly into a yes/no answer without eliciting more follow-up questions, each more intrusive than the last and, by the end, you're giving an oral autobiography to a stranger you just met. The process of seeking refuge and being classified as a refugee is, to say the least, technical, administratively burdensome, and culturally inconsiderate. For example, there is great interest in dates and bloodlines, which are not culturally universal.

This might be tricky to understand, so let me give you some examples of sections of the forms we couldn't quite fill in because our culture simply didn't work that way.

> *It's similar to the way that entrée, main, and dessert cannot simply be translated into different languages because three-course meals is a way of eating that some parts of the world don't have.*

Let me clarify: my mother was born in rural Tigray in her parents' house with a local midwife. Her birth wasn't recorded by the state or her parents. They counted the days to her christening and enrolled her in school when she turned seven. Schools asked about her age, but were never given a date of birth. As she progressed through her adult years, birthdates become even less and less important. So, she filled out an age that she thought was accurate and chose a birth date she felt she could remember for the migration interview. When we went back to visit from Australia, her siblings were all approximating based on what holiday was around her birth, leaving her with a five-year window. Of course, city births were different, but not too different, in my mother's generation.

Another element those forms are obsessed with is our family relations. Is Alem your sister, half-sister, adoptive sister, or stepsister? That's not how our community works. People's siblings are not limited by their biological lineage. In fact, people find it offensive if you break it down to those labels. Alem is just your sister and no one asks for the confirmation of this. There are also many informal adoptions. Although my mom came back to get me after I stayed with my aunt, it wouldn't have been considered unreasonable if she hadn't.

Then we would have to contort our names to fit on those English forms that didn't quite translate. We are left with our father's names as a middle name and our paternal grandfather as our last name. So, you see when you ask migration questions you are asking much more than a yes/no answer that can be tied up neatly with a bow.

> *Tegaru in Khartoum view their life as "in transit," and they are often waiting for their immigration papers to come through from various countries. You go to the relevant offices to see if your name has been posted or wait for your sponsor to call the neighbor's phone to tell you you have been accepted.*

Before people migrated, there was always a big send-off party. Those leaving would get new clothes, give away belongings, and collect spices to take to the new world. People would come around in the final months before their departure and press letters into their palms, entrusting them to give them to friends who had already migrated. People tried to steal my mom into different corners to remind her of their friendship, experiences, and retelling their circumstances, asking her not to forget them, see if she could sponsor them or send money for a medical condition they want to get treated, and so on and so forth.

> *Some parents reminded me how great a friend their kid was to me and not to forget them when I got to Australia. We would promise we wouldn't be like previous people who had left and forgotten them. They would agree and plead, knowing well that most likely we wouldn't see each other again and that we would live in absolute luxury.*

The issue wasn't that people forgot, but that there were too many to remember and they could only just keep their heads above water once they arrived in Australia, while their families back in Tigray also expected help. Therefore, slowly migrants stopped writing letters and calling friends. There were just too many and life in Australia was much harder than they had expected.

DABO KOLO ዳቦ ቆሎ *Fried bread snack*

V VG

Makes 1 lb 2 oz–1 lb 10 oz (500–750 g)

The direct translation for this would be fried bread. I am not sure how it was developed, but this was a snack that was made for going away parties, with kilograms of it being prepared to take overseas with whoever was migrating.

INGREDIENTS

2 cups (300 g) all-purpose flour, plus extra for dusting

½ cup (60 g) confectioners' sugar

1 teaspoon salt

1 teaspoon red food coloring

1 teaspoon yellow food coloring

¼ cup (60 ml) olive oil

sunflower oil, for frying

METHOD

Equally divide the flour, sugar, salt, and ⅓ cup (85 ml) of water between two bowls and mix well.

To one of the bowls, add the red food coloring and to the other, the yellow. Gradually mix in more water if you need it, until you have a thick dough.

Place one of the mixtures on a floured board and knead until you have a stiff ball of dough.

Make an indent in the center of the dough ball and pour in half the olive oil. Fold the dough over the oil and knead for another 5 minutes. Cover with a cloth to keep it moist.

Repeat this process with the other bowl of mixture, using the other half of the olive oil.

Break off chunks of dough and roll into smaller balls, then roll into long, thin strips (like fat spaghetti) using your hands. Cut these strips into ½ inch (1 cm) pieces using scissors or a knife.

Heat enough sunflower oil for deep-frying in a deep heavy-based pot or wok. Using a strainer, carefully spoon the dough pieces into the oil and fry until the color deepens, it shouldn't take longer than 5 minutes per batch. Strain them out of the oil and place on paper towels to drain.

Once cool, store the dabo kolo in an airtight container in a cool, dry area. They will last for months.

MY MOM BUTCHERED A HEN IN AN APARTMENT

The pinnacle of all dishes that shows a Tigraweyti woman's prowess is Dorho sebhi (page 147). This dish is prepared when you have special guests or during celebratory occasions.

Traditionally, the dish takes all day to prepare. The chicken is purchased alive, killed, defeathered, skinned, and divided into 13 pieces. Always 13! Bet you're racking your brain trying to work out how a chicken can be split into so many pieces and this I shall list after the recipe.

Tegaru moms have this obsession that ingredients in the West lack the depth of taste they remember back home. There was a period where my mom was obsessed with the idea that chicken from the butcher's shop was simply not the same. According to her investigations, she felt the taste was being changed at the butchering stage.

To rectify this, she dragged me to Queen Victoria Market in Melbourne to buy a live chicken. I protested in vain, bringing up the logistical challenges of taking a chicken home on the tram. She looked at me steadily and said she had seen cats and dogs on public transport before. I tried to explain to her that cats and dogs are different from chickens. This explanation was outside the logic of my mother's understanding of the animal kingdom hierarchy. I saw it was a losing battle and gave up.

We had been in Australia for two years at that time, but I had taken on the role as the family interpreter all on Year 5 English skills, accumulated in record time. (They never quite taught me enough English to deal with immigration though.)

I hated going to the market with my mom. She liked to go to every aisle, investigate every fruit, and cross-compare prices from at least four stalls before going back and buying it from the first stall we saw.

As we walked through the live animals section, the vendors were telling us about how many eggs the chickens could lay and information about pet maintenance. My mother was insisting I ask questions about the taste of the meat. I had learned enough to know that these chickens were not being sold for dorho sebhi and kept selectively interpreting conversations in an attempt to contain my absolute embarrassment while silently wishing I had Alana's mom, who cooked sausages and mashed potatoes.

Once the transaction was complete, we took the chicken back on the number 57 tram as I prayed to all the gods that no one I knew would see me.

The next day I woke up to a decapitated hen running around our tiny yard waiting to be put out of its misery. I just hoped that the apartments on the second floor wouldn't look down into our yard. As a child born and raised in Sudan, I had no romantic ideas of where the plastic-wrapped meat in the supermarket came from, or what butchering looked like. I had seen farm-to-plate once or twice. My only anxiety was that our neighbors might think we were savages.

My mother had no care in the world and kept asking me to get her lemons, a different knife, a jug of water, and so on as she sat in the courtyard defeathering and sectioning the chicken all day with the onions sautéing in the kitchen.

She was pleased with herself when she served dinner that night and even invited a friend of hers so she could brag how it was all made from scratch. Her friend told her that it was illegal to butcher your own animals in Australia, and got her so paranoid that we bagged all the feathers and distributed them at midnight among all the trash cans that lined the street.

And when Miss Eva asked the class on Monday to write what we did over the weekend? I wrote a flowery imaginary story about how we went to a beach town in Victoria I'd only seen in pictures.

My mother never cooked dorho sebhi from scratch again. She admitted years later that she couldn't tell the difference and it wasn't worth the hassle. I guess the taste she was trying to experience was that of home. The issue wasn't the chicken per se, but the cultural dislocation.

DORHO SEBHI ዶርሆ ፀብሒ

Chicken stew

GF

Traditionally, a whole chicken separated into pieces served with 12 eggs. Why the eggs? The short answer is: no idea. I have asked this question of my mother and all the Tegaru I know. The answer has always been a flaky one at best—along the lines of, "Dorho sebhi has no charisma without the eggs." That's the thing about Tegaru: the culture is passed from one generation to the next with minimal questions but precise implementation. My mom is always perplexed by the questions I ask. It is considered an honor to take this dish to newlyweds.

DORHO SEBHI ዶርሆ ፀብሒ

Chicken stew

GF

Serves 4

INGREDIENTS

8 extra-large chicken drumsticks, skin removed

juice of 2–3 lemons, plus extra if needed

2–4 tablespoons salt, plus extra to taste

8 onions, finely diced

sunflower or vegetable oil, for cooking

4 garlic cloves, minced

7 oz (200 g) Dilik *(page 25)*

2¼ oz (60 g) Tesmi *(page 26)*

6 eggs, hardboiled and peeled

Injera *(page 21)*, **rice or flatbread, to serve**

METHOD

Use a small knife to remove the tendons and stringy parts that are found on the surface of raw chicken. As you gently run the knife across the drumstick, the stringy bits should transfer to your knife. Continue this process until you feel you have removed all these bits.

Then it is traditional to wash the chicken well: Submerge it in room-temperature water with the juice of 1 lemon and 1 tablespoon of salt. Use your hands to wash each piece and, once the water gets murky, empty it out and repeat until the water runs clear. Once the water is clear, submerge the chicken in room-temperature water with more lemon wedges and set aside.

Sauté the onion in a large heavy-bottomed stockpot over low heat with just enough oil to stop it sticking.

Once the onions are brown, add the garlic and stir, then add the dilik. Dilik has a tendency to stick, so you may need to keep stirring and add some water if it begins to stick too much. To avoid diluting the flavor, you want to avoid adding too much water. You are better adding a bit here and there only when needed. Cook the dilik for at least 20 minutes. The longer you cook it the better the flavor will be. As you cook it, the different smells of dilik and onion should merge into one and you should see a deep crimson color.

Drain the chicken and add it to the silsi (that's what the base is called). Stir it through and add enough fresh water to submerge the chicken in the pot. After 10 minutes, add the tesmi.

Put the lid on and stir intermittently to ensure the chicken is coated and cooks evenly. You will know when the chicken is cooked as the meat attached to the bone on the drumstick will start to separate just a tad. This should take about 20 minutes. At this point, add more salt to taste, using the stew to gauge the flavor.

Put the peeled eggs in a serving bowl and add the cooked chicken. Traditionally, this is eaten on a bed of injera, but you can also eat it with rice or flatbread.

I guess by now I ought to tell you how one chicken is separated into thirteen pieces. Well, you have two drumsticks, two thighs, two breasts, two wings, the back is broken in two, then you have the neck, ribs, and the skin. Also, traditionally, the back is given to the man of the house and wings to the kids. Once again, don't ask me why!

- If you find this dish too spicy, serve it with some Greek-style yogurt on the side.

SALATA DAKWA *Peanut butter salad*

GF V VG

Serves 2

This is great condiment for spicy dishes due to the creamy nature of the peanut butter. I also like to add hardboiled eggs and have it as a salad in its own right.

INGREDIENTS

SALAD

2 tomatoes, diced into ½ inch (1 cm) cubes

1 cucumber, peeled or skin on, diced into ½ inch (1 cm) cubes

7 oz (200 g) mixed salad greens, finely shredded

½ green chile, deseeded and finely chopped

DRESSING

juice of 1 lemon

2 tablespoons smooth peanut butter

heaped 1 tablespoon extra virgin olive oil

3 tablespoons water

salt

METHOD

Place all the dressing ingredients in a bowl and mix until you achieve a mayonnaise-like consistency. Season with salt.

Combine the salad ingredients, add the dressing, and mix well to serve.

Opening a restaurant with my mom as head chef

People always ask me why I chose to open a restaurant. I didn't have a grand reason. It was something I fell into, with my mom being the backbone and many others being foundational pillars.

> *The dream was ignited when I would drag different guests to my mom's house for dinner and they would rant and rave how she should open a restaurant.*

I was 25 years old, with a meager budget of $20,000 but full of boundless confidence, a great deal of ingenuity, loved ones who believed in me passionately, truckloads of luck, and a supportive landlord. I signed the lease and expected to launch within six weeks. Everyone looked at me like I was on a different planet. Opening any later was not an option; I only negotiated four weeks rent-free and had a tiny budget. It did help that the venue had been a restaurant before, so no fundamental renovations were needed. The fact that I opened in one of the most competitive hospitality strips in Melbourne was also not a calculated choice, but random. I wanted an existing restaurant and needed a landlord who would be willing to take a chance on me.

One aspect of my ingenuity was the way I laboriously ran around auction houses of failed restaurants leasing equipment instead of purchasing it. Given more than 60 percent of restaurants go out of business in the first year, you can imagine there's an abundance of remnants of culinary dreams.

I had worked for a short period of time as a waitress in my teens and my mother had worked as a kitchen hand and as a home cook for years. I am not sure that we had the experience to run a restaurant, but we definitely had the heart, and I had a mother who had an instinctive hawk eye for waste minimization.

> *We opened to a fully booked restaurant for the first two weeks. The essential element was that the restaurant would simply be an extension of my mom's kitchen, making no modifications to how she cooked for us.*

There was pressure to make our food the way other Ethiopian restaurants did. When we opened the restaurant, just like when we started this book, I called it Saba's Ethiopian Restaurant. This was predominantly a marketing choice. Ethiopian cuisine, as a whole, has penetrated Western dining, so people know what to expect. But we expressed our ethnic identity by writing the menu in Tigrinya and highlighting our culture within the space: we were Tegaru before we were Ethiopian. However, given the current war in the region and my aunts, uncles, and cousins who are caught up in it, I consider it would be a betrayal to my people to call myself Ethiopian anymore. It's now an alien identity to me.

As I've mentioned, the concept of a three-course meal is not a part of the Tigrayan dining experience. The way we serve food is simply by presenting a banquet of everything and letting you fix yourself a plate, or it is presented on a communal platter with all the selections on it. People were always questioning this factor, wanting to make the cuisine fit into the eating format they understood. Given my mother is not a Western-trained chef, I started to take her to various restaurants to inspire some fusion and, from this, Tekebash's cauliflower recipe was born!

TEKEBASH'S CAULIFLOWER

Fried cauliflower

GF V

Serves 2

INGREDIENTS

SALAD

1 cauliflower head

2¾ oz (80 g) Shiro powder *(page 40)*

1 teaspoon salt

½ cup (80 g) rice flour

¼ cup (40 g) teff flour, or flour of your choice

sunflower oil, for deep-frying

DIP

1¾ oz (50 g) blue cheese

½ cup (100 g) mayonnaise

½ teaspoon minced garlic

½ teaspoon salt

heaped 1 tablespoon whole milk

METHOD

Break the cauliflower into large florets with your fingers, then remove any large stems. Cut the florets into smaller pieces, approximately ¾–1¼ inches (2–3 cm) in size.

Mix the shiro and salt in a bowl with enough water to make a runny mixture, like a pulpy juice.

Mix the rice flour and teff flour on a tray.

For the blue cheese dip, mix all the ingredients in a food processor and set aside.

Dip the cauliflower florets into the shiro mixture, ensuring the entire floret is dipped. Remove and shake gently to remove excess liquid. You want it to be wet enough to hold the flour but not so wet that it turns your tray of flour into dough.

Roll the cauliflower floret in the flour, tapping it a little to remove excess flour. Let it chill in the fridge for an hour.

Heat enough oil for deep-frying in a wok. The oil should start to form small bubbles. Put the heat on high and then reduce to medium once the oil is ready. Fry the cauliflower until golden brown. You may need to turn it to ensure equal frying on all sides.

Drain on paper towels to remove any excess oil, then serve with the blue cheese dip.

KATANIA ቃጠኛ *Chile toastie*

GF V

Serves 4

This is a snack that is usually served while someone is making injera.

INGREDIENTS

heaped 1 tablespoon Dilik *(page 25)*

heaped 1 tablespoon Tesmi *(page 26)*

2 room-temperature Injera *(page 21)*

salt

METHOD

In a bowl, combine the dilik and tesmi, season with salt to taste, and mix until it is the consistency of thick peanut butter.

Spread the mixture on half of each injera. If you spread it everywhere, it will fall apart when you toast it.

Fold the injera in half and place it in a hot sandwich press or toaster oven for 10 seconds.

Take it out and cut into quarters to serve.

Raising a child through a tea cart

When my mother was left as a single mother in Sudan, she needed to work out how to provide for us really quickly. Returning to be a maid wasn't viable as most maids were live-in and required to stay with the family six days a week. So, the best option was for my mom to be a street vendor.

> *She would sell tea, coffee, and popsicles from the veranda of our house. Many habesha women sold tea and coffee from the side of the street and in front of office buildings.*

This was a relatively accessible business with minimal fixed costs, thus minimal financial risk. This also allowed women to choose their hours, which made it easier with childrearing.

Most of these street vendors never had the appropriate paperwork, as that would have created a barrier to entry they couldn't overcome. This made street vendors a combination of legal business holders and illegal vendors.

> *At times, the police would crack down and confiscate their entire set-up and they would have to start again.*

The streets of Khartoum were peppered with habesha women sitting behind their tea carts.

SHAHI *Spiced black tea*

GF V VG

Serves 4-6

You can make a traditional habesha digestive tea by adding a shot of ouzo. Ouzo, called areki or arek in Tigray, is used as a digestive after a heavy meat meal. Despite popular conception, ouzo/areki extends beyond the Greek culture and is enjoyed by various countries in Eastern Europe and is very popular in Ethiopia.

INGREDIENTS

1 teaspoon whole cloves

1 teaspoon whole cardamom pods

2 large cinnamon sticks, broken into pieces

heaped 1 tablespoon white sugar

1 oz (30 g) loose-leaf black tea *(see tip)*

METHOD

Lightly crush the cloves and cardamom to release more flavor.

Put all the spices and sugar in a stovetop teapot with 4¼ cups (1 liter) of water, and place over low heat. Bring it to a simmer. Try to keep it on the heat for a minimum of 15 minutes.

Add the tea leaves and boil for 1 more minute. Use a tea strainer and pour into a mug.

- Simple black tea is best for a stronger flavor. If you can't get loose leaf, you can use 3 to 5 tea bags. Putting the tea in too early or leaving it too long will create a bitter taste.

SHAHI BE LEBEN *Spiced milk tea*

GF V

Serves 4-6

This is like a masala chai or chai latte. It tastes better the longer you brew it, but also works in quick time. Khartoum has a huge tea culture with street sellers at every corner. I guess it's a blend of the British colonial history and the Arab influence.

A shot of Amarula will make this a lovely adult drink. Amarula is a liqueur from South Africa. Although similar to Baileys, it has a peachy, earthy flavor. This is most certainly not traditional, but rather something we created for after-work drinks influenced by Irish coffee.

INGREDIENTS

1 teaspoon whole cloves

1 teaspoon whole cardamom pods

4¼ cups (1 liter) whole milk

1 oz (30 g) loose-leaf black tea *(see tip)*

2 large cinnamon sticks, broken into pieces

3 tablespoons white sugar

METHOD

Lightly crush the cloves and cardamom to release more flavor.

Place all the ingredients in a stovetop teapot and bring to a low simmer. If you don't have a stovetop teapot you can use a saucepan with a handle. You will need to remove the lid to stir it once in a while to stop overflow.

Try to keep it on the flame for a minimum of 15 minutes. Despite the fact that this may cook super quickly, the longer you give it the tastier it gets.

Pour through a tea strainer into mugs.

- Simple black tea is best for a stronger flavor. If you can't get loose leaf, you can use 3 to 5 tea bags. Choose a milk alternative with a mild flavor to make this vegan friendly.

From left to right: Entatie (page 168), Shahi (page 164), Shahi be leben (page 165), Mes (page 169)

ENTATIE እንጣጢዕ *Flaxseed juice*

GF V

Serves 2

This is an acquired taste! The granulated texture in the mouth can be tricky. I am not a major fan of it but my mother loves it. She also raves about the digestive health qualities.

INGREDIENTS

3 tablespoons flaxseeds

1⅔ cups (400 ml) water

honey or sugar, to taste

METHOD

In a dry frying pan, toast the flaxseeds for 30 seconds to 1 minute. Take off the heat and transfer to a bowl to cool. When cool, grind the flaxseeds with a spice grinder or mortar and pestle.

In a blender, combine the ground seeds with the water and the honey to taste. Blend for 5 seconds.

Serve and drink soon after. If it has been sitting for a while, give it a quick stir before drinking.

MES ሜስ *Homemade honey wine*

GF V

Serves around 10

In Tigray there are two traditional alcoholic beverages that are made. One is called sewa and the other is mes. Sewa is a beverage made from dates and barley that is drunk daily. There isn't really an age limit, and even young children drink it. This might be due to the lack of clean drinking water—it provides a safer option.

Mes, however, is more of a special drink made for celebrations. It can range from beer strength to vodka strength depending on how long you leave it for; use a hydrometer before and after fermentation if you want to know how strong it is! There are bars in Tigray that sell only sewa or mes. You can double this recipe if you like.

INGREDIENTS

3 cups (1 kg) pure honey (the ratio of honey to water is 1:4)

1 gallon (4 liters) filtered water

1½ teaspoons (4 g) instant yeast

small handful of geysho leaves (these can be found at any habesha grocery)

heaped 1 teaspoon ground turmeric

METHOD

Mix the honey with the filtered water, yeast, and geysho leaves in a large tub with a tight-fitting lid. If you cannot find whole leaves, use crushed leaves and place them in a stocking or cheesecloth bag. Tie well before putting it in the tub.

In a cup, mix the turmeric with a small amount of water until well combined, then add this to the tub.

Check to see the color is a nice golden yellow and is slightly transparent. Seal the tub and let it sit for 3–4 weeks, until the taste and strength is to your liking (the timing can vary depending on the weather).

An attempt at dessert and the blending of cultures

Tigray cuisine doesn't have a dessert offering in the sense that Western cuisine does. Meals are usually ended with traditional coffee or tea accompanied by salted popcorn.

The meals may be followed by himbasha, or roasted grains and nuts; however, these aren't particularly sweet. Country folk who keep bees might have fresh honeycomb. City folk might serve fruit—a specialty for the area is prickly pear. It is delicate to unfurl but the flesh is sweet.

The kind-of desserts in this book are a mix of traditions, as are my mom's take on lasagne and the beer-soaked barbecue rub that follow. An ultimately delicious melting pot.

HIMBASHA ሕምባሻ *Focaccia*

V VG

Makes a 9–10 inch (22–25 cm) "cake"

When we were kids growing up in Australia, my mom would keep calling this Tigray's cake, though it's actually more like focaccia. Given that most of our diet is spicy, I guess neutral is a cake. Traditionally we only celebrate first birthdays. When a child turns one, a himbasha would be broken in half on their back, with the idea of strengthening their back. Maybe this is why my mom feels it's a cake equivalent.

INGREDIENTS

4 cups (500 g) bread flour or all-purpose flour

½ tablespoon salt

1⅔ teaspoons (5 g) instant yeast

½ teaspoon black sesame seeds

2 tablespoons sunflower or vegetable oil

cooking oil spray

METHOD

Put all the dry ingredients into a bowl and mix well. Add the sunflower oil to the mixture.

Gradually add water, kneading as you go, until you achieve a dough. Knead the dough for 10–15 minutes.

Cover the bowl and let it sit for 2 hours in a warm place so the mixture can rise.

Once risen to at least 1½ times to double the size, line a baking sheet with foil and spray the foil with cooking oil.

Preheat the oven to 350°F (180°C). Put the dough on the tray and shape it with your hands into a 9–10 inch (22–25 cm) round.

Traditionally, we use the edges of a fork or knife to create a personalized design.

Bake for 20–30 minutes. You will know it is ready when the smell fills up the whole house. Use a toothpick to check it is cooked in 5 minute intervals, commencing at 20 minutes. If the toothpick comes out clean, it is cooked.

Traditionally this is eaten as an accompaniment to tea or coffee. However, it is a great base for toasted sandwiches or even for eating with stews.

VEGAN TEFF ANZAC-LIKE COOKIES

GF V VG

Makes 8–10

When I was 22 I imported one tonne of teff flour to sell. My inspiration for this was a couple of vegan blogs that recommended asking "Ethiopian" friends to source this obscure superfood that was going to be the next quinoa. I faced an enormous challenge moving this much product and, as a result, I began a very brief baking career making "Anzac" cookies. I started selling them at farmers' markets and to health-food stores until one lovely lady told me calling them Anzac was illegal. So I quickly stopped selling them before the Department of Veterans' Affairs got onto me and now we call them Anzac-like.

INGREDIENTS

½ cup (75 g) teff flour

½ cup (110 g) brown sugar

1 gluten-free Weetabix (or ¾ oz/20 g gluten-free toasted oats or shredded wheat cereal), crushed to a similar size as oats

¼ cup (25 g) shredded coconut

⅓ cup (75 g) margarine

heaped 1 tablespoon rice malt syrup

¼ teaspoon gluten-free baking powder

METHOD

Preheat the oven to 350°F (180°C).

Sift the flour into a bowl, then add the sugar, Weetabix, and the coconut.

Melt the margarine in a saucepan and add the rice malt syrup, baking powder, and 2 teaspoons of water.

Add the liquid to the dry ingredients and mix thoroughly. I use a tablespoon and it seems to do the job. However, you can use a food processor.

The mixture will have texture, but you should still be able to bind it together. Scoop up a heaped 1 tablespoon of the mixture and place it on a greased baking sheet. Repeat with the rest of the mixture, then bake for about 17 minutes.

Let the cookies cool down before serving; they won't harden until they cool down.

I have kept these in an airtight container for up to 2 weeks. They don't spoil, but can become quite hard.

MOM'S LASAGNE

I am not sure how this recipe came about, but mom always seemed responsible for bringing lasagne to people's houses at some point. While working as a kitchenhand in restaurants, she had taken to looking at the recipes that came home with the supermarket flyers, but never following them. She took them as a guide and came up with her own interpretations. That's why I had to follow her around the kitchen like a hawk to write this recipe book. She understood the need for people to know the ingredients and steps, but as for measurements, well, she thought that was just a tastebuds thing. >

MOM'S LASAGNE

Serves 8

INGREDIENTS

3 onions, finely diced

⅔ cup (150 ml) sunflower or olive oil, plus extra for cooking

8 garlic cloves, peeled

2 x 14 oz (400 g) cans Italian diced tomatoes

3 tablespoons chopped parsley

bunch of fresh rosemary sprigs, leaves stripped and finely chopped, or a heaped 1 tablespoon dried rosemary

1 lb 2 oz (500 g) lean ground beef

2 teaspoons salt, plus extra to taste

1⅔ cups (200 g) all-purpose flour

2½ cups (600 ml) whole milk

½ teaspoon freshly ground black pepper

butter, for greasing

1 lb 2 oz (500 g) dry lasagne sheets

1¾ cups (200 g) shredded four-cheese blend

METHOD

Start by making a bolognese sauce. Sauté the onion in a little oil in a pot over medium heat until translucent, then add the garlic and cook for another minute. Add the tomato.

Add the parsley and rosemary and let it simmer for 15 minutes. Turn off the heat and set aside.

In a separate pot over low heat, put a tablespoon of oil and the ground beef and stir for 10 minutes, or until the meat has browned and cooked through.

Return the tomato sauce to medium heat and transfer the beef to the pot. Add 1 teaspoon of the salt and cook for 5–10 minutes. Taste the bolognese and add more salt if needed. Set aside.

Next, make a béchamel: Toast the flour in a dry nonstick frying pan over low heat. Take it off the heat and set aside.

In a saucepan, heat the sunflower oil and wait for it to bubble up a little. Slowly add the toasted flour, stirring continuously, then gradually stir in the milk. Continue to stir until you've poured all the milk into the pot. The consistency should be like thick soup. If it's not, add some more water. When the milk begins to bubble, add the remaining teaspoon of salt and the pepper.

Let it cook for 10 minutes over low heat and then set aside.

Preheat the oven to 350°F (180°C). Grease a 7 x 12 inch (18 x 30 cm) baking dish with butter.

Put a layer of the bolognese sauce in the base of the dish, then top with lasagne sheets, followed by a layer of béchamel. Repeat this pattern until you get to the top of the dish. Put some béchamel and bolognese together on the final layer.

Add the shredded cheese on top. Bake for 30–40 minutes, or until the cheese forms a crisp outer layer. Check to make sure the lasagne is cooked by prodding with a fork in the center. Set aside to cool a little, then serve.

- Instead of cheese, you can whisk two eggs and pour this on the top layer. I'm not sure how my mom came across this solution, but nonetheless there it is.

BARBECUE RUB

Well, if nothing else, Australians (predominantly the Caucasian ones) will tell you there is nothing more Australian than barbecuing. As my family began to create a unique blend of Tigrayan Australian culture, barbecues became a part of our family gatherings. They didn't start because we had a need to eat barbecued food per se, but rather because my mother preferred to wash less and prepare food in less time. As you might have noticed, most of the dishes in this book require a fair bit of chopping, sautéing, and so on. Throwing a lamb rib on a public barbecue at Footscray Park? Now that's efficient.

Why does my mom use Victoria Bitter? Well, surprisingly Victoria Bitter and Carlton Draught were extremely popular within the Tigrayan community, just like every fridge only had Pura milk. The popularity of these brands had nothing to do with preference. The decision-making process within the community when it came to buying items they weren't acquainted with was to buy whatever you saw at the first house you landed in when you came to Australia. From this, what you got was a whole community that had brand loyalty based on what they initially saw. ›

LAMB CHOPS WITH BARBECUE RUB

Serves 10

INGREDIENTS

1¼ inch (3 cm) piece ginger, peeled and crushed

6 garlic cloves, peeled

5 tablespoons lemon pepper

heaped 1 tablespoon Dilik *(page 25)*

juice of 1 lemon

1½ cups (375 ml) Victoria Bitter lager, other lager, or non-alcoholic ginger beer

4 lb 8 oz (2 kg) lamb chops (fat on)

Awaze *(page 75)*, **to serve**

salt

METHOD

Crush the ginger and garlic together in a bowl, then add the lemon pepper and dilik.

Add the lemon juice and salt to taste. Next, add the beer and stir until you have a runny, smooth consistency. Add the lamb and turn to coat evenly. Refrigerate overnight or for 2–3 hours at least.

Heat a barbecue grill to high and cook the lamb for 5 minutes on each side, or until a little charred (or cooked to your preference).

Rest the meat for a few minutes and serve the finished lamb with Awaze or condiments of your choice.

CELIAC-SAFE RESTAURANT

One of the key decisions I made before opening the restaurant was that I wanted it to be completely celiac safe. This decision was a personal one.

My younger sister was diagnosed with celiac disease when she was four years old. We were lucky that she received a diagnosis so early, though the way it came about was traumatic to say the least.

I remember the day clearly: I was helping Mom wake her up to go to daycare. She opened her eyes, but her body was limp. Mom tried to get her up to stand on the bed and she wouldn't hold her body up, despite her eyes being open. My mother screamed, I ran into the room and tried to get her alert too. I was around 16 years old. It was the strangest thing to watch when someone is there but can't move a limb at all; she was just dead weight. We rushed to the hospital and, of course, being the family interpreter I was trying to explain our experience while they asked weird questions that I translated to my mom.

The doctors kept asking me obscure questions that implied neglect by our family. Even though I answered (like the good interpreter I was), I would tell my mom the parts of the questions she missed, and she would yell at me like I had asked these things.

So, we found out that my sister was malnourished, as her body wasn't able to process the food she was eating because it had gluten in it, and it had also caused some kind of damage to her stomach lining.

My sister was a thin child and mealtimes were always stressful. She would refuse to eat, screaming at whoever was feeding her and then vomiting almost every second meal once the last spoonful had gone into her mouth.

I had been exactly the same, without the vomiting, and I had no issues, so my mom thought, "Here is take two of Saba." My mom did bring up her slimness with our family doctor and she was told she was on the smaller side but nothing of significance and she will grow out of her eating problems.

This was in early 2000s before gluten-free eating had become so common. So we commenced our label-reading and predominantly cooking from scratch. We didn't need to significantly change our diet as we discovered most traditional dishes were inherently gluten-free anyway.

> *One of the things that was challenging was that we could never eat out stress-free without fear of cross-contamination. Secondly, it was always agonising for my sister, who was a bit young to constantly be missing out.*

DECONSTRUCTED SAMOSAS

GF V VG

Why do you make it deconstructed? Well, running a restaurant with your mother is challenging enough without you giving her the impossible task of folding gluten-free pastry without it falling apart. Samosas, although not traditionally Tigrayan, have become a popular snack and street food influenced by returnees from South Asia, the Middle East, and North Africa. The filling is different to the traditional recipe as we usually use the green lentil stew (page 116) made thicker, or spiced meat.

We discovered early on that Australians don't quite love legumes the way we do. But given we were a celiac-safe restaurant and had to use gluten-free pastry, getting it to stick together was near impossible. And just like that, out of necessity and without knowing him from a bar of soap, my mom took inspiration from chef Ferran Adrià. Deconstructed samosas were born, mother–daughter relationship intact. >

DECONSTRUCTED SAMOSAS

GF V VG

Serves 8

INGREDIENTS

1 small onion, finely diced

oil, for cooking and deep-frying

1 teaspoon freshly minced garlic

1 teaspoon ground turmeric

½ teaspoon ground cumin

2 carrots, finely diced

1 cup (155 g) peas

¼ green or white cabbage, finely shredded

2 sheets gluten-free puff pastry (at room temperature)

salt

METHOD

Sauté the onion in a frying pan over medium heat with just enough oil to stop it sticking. When the onion starts to brown and become translucent, add the garlic and sauté for another minute or so.

Add the turmeric and cumin, stir, then add a bit of water so the mixture looks like a paste.

Add the carrot and cook for less than 5 minutes until al dente. Then add the peas and cook for approximately 2 minutes. Add the shredded cabbage and season with salt. Cook until the cabbage begins to wilt, then take it off the heat and set aside.

Cut each puff pastry sheet into 16 triangles. You can do this by cutting in a cross motion through the center vertically and horizontally. Then cut from corner to corner in each square, giving you four triangles.

Heat enough oil for deep-frying in a deep pan or wok. Carefully place as many triangles as you can in the oil without them touching. Turn the pastry when it becomes golden brown, then transfer to paper towels to drain.

Serve the samosa mixture in a small serving bowl, surrounded by the pastry triangles, and serve with a spoon, similar to how you might serve chips and salsa.

COVID-19

In 2020, Saba's Ethiopian Restaurant was about to hit the elusive milestone of being open for five years.

In March 2020, there were murmurs of a virus coming out of China that would have an impact on Australia. Most of us scoffed that we had been there for Bird Flu or SARS and this was going to be nothing but a flash in the pan. It was Friday March 20th and we had met with the Melbourne Food and Wine curators to discuss me being an ambassador for the event (I had sold out the event I was running two weeks in advance). We spoke about how we believed we could get around the COVID-19 issues with some risk mitigation. The meeting concluded at 3:30 pm and by 5:15 pm I received an email saying everything was getting canceled. The same day, I was notified that other major festivals we had contracts with were also no longer going ahead.

In the first weeks of COVID-19 hitting Melbourne, it was a state of absolute mental chaos. We all became scientists overnight, which didn't help matters.

Event after event was canceled and refunds were processed irrespective of the expenses already incurred. I just wanted the ground to open up and swallow me. I had no idea what to do and found all conversations created a cyclone of anxiety. People would hypothesize, minimize, and smother others with their supposed moral superiority and neat slogans, such as "Stay home, save lives," and news channels would run repetitive coverage centered around what they didn't know about the virus.

I would cry as I pounded the pavement for my daily runs. I felt like this was the only thing that would help me cope. Then there was the "we are in it together" bandwagon—wasn't that a scam! I've never felt more isolated than those days. It affected all of us differently to varying degrees.

Then the announcement was made that restaurants could only do delivery or takeout. Prior to COVID, only five percent of our business was based on delivery and takeout. Well, we pivoted to survival mode with the intention of holding on for the six months we expected it to last. I remember a mentor telling me that big businesses are planning for six months, so I accepted this challenge and embarked on the six months with toxic positivity and scrambled after every press conference. When we reopened, it was the first time I'd spent money on advertising and promoting, only to be closed in a snap lockdown just weeks later.

> *COVID wasn't just impacting small businesses financially, but also psychologically, as those business owners suddenly found themselves working in an environment they'd never signed up for.*

As soon as the second lockdown happened, I ran up the white flag. I didn't want my business to survive; it was too hard, too much. The press conferences were exhausting: everyone's "How is lockdown?" conversations were repetitive. Being in a people-facing business meant I had no mental energy to cope with the hardship, but had to find extra to pour into our customers. The reason for opening the business no longer felt valid. We were now operating an empty space at a daily loss. As soon as the second lockdown happened, I knew that it would be years before Melbourne went back to normal and I didn't want to soldier through it.

Making the decision to close was a relief and a bit exciting. People's reaction to the decision felt extremely overwhelming. I appreciated that it was disappointing for them, but the emotional labor of dealing with their feelings was tougher than my choice to close the doors on our terms.

> *There was an element of "even if we survive this, will the landscape be what we signed up for?" We were completely demotivated to come in, day in, day out, to an empty restaurant, pack takeout containers, and try to deliver within a five kilometer (three mile) radius.*

This in itself was fatiguing! We had an excellent run and a great time, but we were content to stop our journey there.

I am people-centric and passionate about my heritage and creating spaces that bring people together. I don't have a pedantic commitment to the format that comes in. I am just happy to share these recipes with you for your dinner table, or host pop-ups and beyond.

> *I opened a restaurant to invite Melbourne into my mom's kitchen. Now we write this cookbook to give you a window into the rich heritage of Tigray and a mother-daughter duo who call it home.*

MENU IDEAS

This food is made to be shared with others, and to allow you to have variety on your table without too much excess.

CASUAL BUFFET DINNER

For 10

The best thing about this menu is that you are able to make everything in advance before your guests arrive; just leave the salad dressing on the side. You will be the host with the most.

1. **Bamya** 63
2. **Dorho sebhi** 147
3. **Salata dakwa** 153
4. **Dinish** 124
5. **Injera** 21
6. **Ruz** 64

CHILDREN FRIENDLY MENU

For 8

Some spices can be challenging to palates not accustomed to them. These selections give little ones bright colors and no chile as a great introduction to Tigrayan cuisine. The eating-with-fingers part is also a hit.

1. **Deconstructed samosas** 189
2. **Dinish** 124
3. **Defun birsen** 116
4. **Derek kulwa** 77
5. **Injera** 21
6. **Ruz** 64

>

VEGAN BONANZA

For 6

Tigray's cuisine is basically vegan heaven and this menu is the quintessential vegan dinner party.

1. **Birsen** 115
2. **Hamli** 120
3. **Duba** 127
4. **Alicha birsen** 119
5. **Injera** 21

BRUNCH

For 6

This is my absolute favorite, as it brings back all the nostalgia of Khartoum. I would highly recommend preparing some elements ahead, such as the tamia mix.

1. **Ful** 91
2. **Tamia** 93
3. **Semek** 97
4. **Himbasha** 173
5. **Shahi** 164

SPECIAL DINNER

For 2

This meal for me hits all the right spots: that slow-cooked protein, dairy, sourdough-style bread, and those beets.

1. **Tekebash's cauliflower** 159
2. **Keyih sebhi** 73
3. **Keysir** 128
4. **Ajebo** 74
5. **Injera** 21

PICNIC MENU

For 6

This was selected based on what keeps outside and for ease of eating. Fire up the grill in your local park.

1. **Fit fit** 57
2. **Lamb chops with barbecue rub** 183
3. **Salata aswad** 92
4. **Salata dakwa** 153
5. **Himbasha** 173
6. **Injera** 21

STOCKISTS

Specialized ingredients can be sourced at African and Afro-Caribbean grocery stores and markets. Many ingredients are also available at healthfood stores and online.

RESOURCES

For those of you who want to know more about the dynamics of the Tegaru people in current-day Ethiopia, I don't have much material I can promote in English. The insular nature of our culture has been against our public relations. I would recommend, however, that you read reputable sources such as *The Economist*, BBC, *The New York Times*, the United Nations website, *Foreign Policy* magazine, *France 24*, Al Jazeera, and the like. They have all covered the current conflict in various degrees and some have provided analysis of how we find ourselves here.

ACKNOWLEDGMENTS

I can't genuinely expect to acknowledge all the people who have made this book possible. The two individuals I am extremely indebted to are my mama, Tekebash, and sister Sara. My mother humored my thoughts of opening a restaurant and even writing this book. She is so humble she doesn't know the impact she made on the Melbourne dining scene. As far as she is concerned she simply cooked in her daughter's restaurant.

My patient sister, at the age of 19, translated most of the recipes between balancing school, work, and the impact of COVID-19. Without her this book wouldn't have been possible.

The family, friends, and my intimate partner who washed dishes for me and ran around picking up ingredients at the last minute. Friends who gave us the opportunity to host/cater their special days, and let's not forget those family and friends I had to kick out because I double-booked their table.

A special thank you to my landlord-turned-mentor, Neil Witchell, who took a chance on an inexperienced 25-year-old restaurateur. I will always be in debt to you.

The customers who turned into friends and family. They invested in us, and we in them. It took a whole community for me to indulge myself in a dream and for that I am thankful.

እንኳዕ ካባኹም ተፈጠርኩ

INDEX

D

E